Seasons & Celebrations

Seasons & Celebrations

Rosalie Fuscaldo Gaziano

PELICAN PUBLISHING COMPANY
GRETNA 1984

First printing, September 1982
Second printing, April 1984

Library of Congress Cataloging in Publication Data

Gaziano, Rosalie Fuscaldo.
  Seasons and celebrations.
  Includes index.
  1. Cookery, Italian. I. Title.
TX723.G33 1984   641.5945'7   84-4226
ISBN 0-88289-443-9 (pbk.)

"Italian Kitchen" reprinted from Russell Marano, *Poems from a Mountain Ghetto* (Webster Springs, West Virginia: Black Fork Books, 1979), by permission of the author.

Book design and title page illustrations by Pat Cahape
Inside illustrations and photographs by Phil Gaziano
Front and back cover photographs by Gary Simmons

Manufactured in the United States of America
Published by Pelican Publishing Company, Inc.
1101 Monroe Street, Gretna, Louisiana 70053

Table of Contents

ITALIAN KITCHEN

Mysterious room
for alchemists of appetites
measurers of
parsley, oregano, bay leaves.

Magic room,
with enormous family table,
filled
with fruits, vegetables, salads,
entrees of
lasagna, baked eel, chicken livers,
Italian sausage, rigatoni and gnocchi.

Largest room
in the house
where simmering tomato sauces,
like seductive perfumes,
titillate enzymes,
starting body juices flowing.

Russell Marano

Introduction

Every reader of a "how-to" book deserves to know the source of the material. In the case of this cookbook, you deserve to know the origin of the recipes and how they will work for you.

This is primarily a family cookbook, based on the original recipes of two families who came from different parts of Italy. My family, from Calabria in southern Italy, and my husband's family, from Aragona in Sicily, add two different dimensions to the book. The third source is the synthesis and expansion of ideas as these recipes are adapted to fit the American scene.

The love of cooking and the art of sharing food began for me in my family home in West Virginia. Growing up surrounded by the sights and smells of a warm kitchen, I learned quickly the kind of spiritual nourishment and special fun that come only from the creating and sharing of good food. Politics were discussed, and problems were solved, as food was prepared. Feelings were soothed as the soup was served, and ideas were passed around with the pasta. Our eyes were delighted with pretty tables and colorful gastronomic creations. I learned that there is more to food than meets the palate.

Both of my grandmothers brought simple recipes and different preparation methods from remote areas of the mysterious Sila Mountains and the olive growing plateaus of southern Italy. My parents, American-born, took the simple ideas and added American touches. So, with a little Yankee ingenuity, Italian ice cream touched off our Fourth of July, and Parmesan dressing oozed from the turkey on Thanksgiving. Our neighborhood would never be the same. At Christmas, friends came by with mincemeat pies and fudge, hoping to be invited in for pita-piata and torrone candy. Sometimes new combinations were born.

My husband's family came from another Italian province across the straits of Messina in Sicily. They kept their dishes pure, for the most part, preferring the slow bubbling of soups to quick American hamburgers. As I came to enjoy their specialties, I saw some possibilities for using them in our American sytle of life. One more dimension was added to our holidays and everyday meals.

The Italians I know are warm and generous people. Our

doors were always open, and as the scents of rich tomatoes and yeast sent out their aromas, many people came in. Friends tasted, enjoyed, and were nourished by our foods. Needless to say, friendships can grow under such conditions. As our friends commented and added their ideas, the recipes were expanded again. When my husband and I traveled and lived in different parts of the United States and Europe, we added other creative touches—a trifle with Italian Marsala, minestrone with New England beans.

And so here we are in the 1980s, with a wealth of Italian ideas, enriched by the American way of life, ready for you to enjoy. The book is divided into seasons, highlighting holidays and seasonal foods of the American culture—foods for homecoming, the Fourth of July, and spring break. The festive spirit of all the dishes demonstrates how you can make a holiday out of any day, with the creative warmth and vitality of Italian ideas.

The Italians, unlike French chefs, do not boast of complicated sauces and ingredients. The Italians wisely use what is available at any given time of year—a ripe tomato, a bit of basil, a young chicken—foods that are economical and full of rich, true flavors. Unlike the bland fast foods plaguing America, these simple foods have the unique quality of good taste.

How do these recipes fit time-conscious, diet-conscious, work-oriented Americans?

The recipes in this book fit you and me perfectly, as busy Americans, because they are simple—a hen in six quarts of water, noodles frozen ahead of time, cheese served simply with good bread. Old, time-consuming methods have been updated and refined to fit our busy schedules. The freezer, the microwave oven, and the charcoal grill can be used with these recipes—but the ingredients, aroma, and tender taste are genuine.

Directions are simple. They could be followed by men and children (our five sons use them), experienced or not, as well as by busy working women. However, the recipes are merely an enticing way to begin—they leave much room for your creativity to flow!

Diet-wise, these recipes are based on simple, good nutrition my physician husband would endorse. The emphasis is on lean meats, simple broths, fresh fruits, and real flavors.

Economy-wise from the beginning, the Italian immigrant brought simple ideas to America: bread, cheese, broth, and tomatoes. These still beat the price at both natural food stores and fast food restaurants. The Italian flair for art makes our red, white, and green dishes festive in appearance. The secret of inexpensive ingredients is using foods at their prime availability. A bunch of broccoli, in season, with a little lemon juice and an egg, is less expensive (and more nutritious) than processed vegetables from the supermarket. There is no economy like buying foods at their peak abundance and using them sensibly.

Americans have grown sophisticated in their tastes—sophisticated enough to know that subtleties are superior to thick coatings and that quality means good foods in their pure forms.

Food, lovingly prepared, is nourishment not only for the body but for the spirit. The spirit of warmth and fullness of taste is the spirit of Italian cooking.

Acknowledgements

A special thanks to my parents for their sense of artful ingenuity in creating foods, and for their spirit of gregarious warmth in the sharing of good food.

To my husband's parents, who lovingly shared their traditional preparations of fine food as well as their warm feelings.

To our many friends and relatives, who expanded the clan's ideas with their individual touches—especially the Fuscaldo, Gango, Gaziano, and Amato families, who form our family tree.

To Carol Paradis, Colleen Anderson, Paula McKenney, Norma Hammons, Franca Martin, Peggy Schultz, who gave their technical knowledge and endless support.

To my husband and five sons, who not only lovingly supported me through the tedious research, but who patiently waited for meals while we photographed them.

Winter

The celebration of Christmas is centered around a Child, and indeed it is a celebration of childhood—the consummate feast of man and child.

My memories of Christmas Past have within them a child's measure of myth, and the warmth of a large Italian clan.

A few traditions and some simple recipes brought from the barren tip of Italy's boot began our Italian-American celebration.

Christmas celebrations outlived death, depression, frugal years, and even family feuds. If there were pennies enough for some flour, some honey, and a little wine, these were combined in the most loving forms to celebrate Natale (The Birth).

And as the flour and wine changed form, the problems of the year were dissolved in the batter. All of it was leavened in the oven—and only the intoxicating flavors and warm tastes were left in the mouth at Christmas. There were many to join in this process, for with the last flush of immigration, the family was big.

In time, my parents moved our little nuclear family away from the seat of the clan—one hour's drive on a winding West Virginia road. But Christmas Eve always found us winding the path back to the heart of the traditional celebration.

It was always a magic drive for us—an hour of anticipating once-a-year foods and once-a-year sights. Electric decorations blinked outside the car windows as we wound around the narrow, hilly slopes. One small town led to another, bleak and coal-striped in November but now transfixed with the magic glow of Christmas lights. The black coal dust was hidden under the precious white snow of December.

When we arrived in Clarksburg, a long progression of visits began. From aunt to aunt, we were greeted by tables already set. There was hardly time to recover from one gastronomical ecstasy before the door was opened on another.

A night of fasting and expectation was really a feast begun. Christmas Eve on the liturgical calendar shows fish and fast, but each "meatless" table was generously laden with a crispy array of assorted fishes, long soaked and now devoid of the odors that must have plagued the neighbors two days before. Beautifully baked and fried, the assorted fishes lay next to companion piles of deep fried fritta (fresh yeast dough) wrapped around salty sardines and anchovies or sprinkled with sugar and honey for the children.

The climax of the magic night was the Midnight Mass, a time when the 13 younger cousins were all clustered in Grandma's house, bedded across the width of a few iron beds in the high-ceilinged, drafty bedrooms.

The grates were turned low and the whispers hushed, but not before a round of guesses about what lay in the parlor below. The glass doors had been shut to our touch; the tall tree protected the tokens beneath that would be waiting for us in the morning.

But clanging sounds came from the kitchen well into the night. Pita-piatas were filled with raisins and nuts and shaped into wreaths. Pizzelles were made on the hot iron. Those who had had a good year in business sent wine and flour; maiden aunts and those with too many children, who had only their hands to give, shaped flour into delicious pastries. On they cooked.

After Midnight Mass, the party continued for the adults. Morning met them merrymaking, having consumed, after Mass, a ham, some gelatin, bowls of Lupini beans, and a few wine-soaked pita balls.

It took the clear broth of delicate chicken soup to cleanse and prepare the stomach for the final, late afternoon meal. It was at this final feast that the red pastas and crisp green salads took their places with the turkey, always followed by mounds of wreath-shaped pita-piatas, crisp bow-shaped pastries, and

round waffle-like pizzelles. These were left out to serve anyone who came to the door on this night of nights.

When we started our own branch of the family, it was impossible to think of Christmas without some sharing of the consummate feast. As we spent years far away from the West Virginia hills and the clan, foods of our cherished childhood became the link to home and family.

When, as students, we huddled in a three-story tenement, there was a Christmas feast shared with our friends. When the family grew from one to five sons, the kitchen was filled with many sticky male hands preparing the celebration of the Birthday Party.

In spirit, the children were reminded to fill an empty crib with straw—a European custom in which each straw represents a good deed, and thus the crib is made soft for the Child.

Meanwhile, we were filling the freezer with foods that had become a tradition for our family. The four weeks of Advent were precious little time to roll and fry and freeze for the final Feast of the year.

When we moved from Richmond in the south to New England, the traditions of America touched our tables. The doors of the world were opened after a year in Europe. Christmas in England found us putting a plum pudding on the table. And always these were accompanied by red pastas and pastries of our past, to keep the link alive.

With love, we have cooked together. Come celebrate the season with us.

Broiled Parmesan Mushrooms

12 large fresh mushrooms
2 tablespoons melted butter
1 tablespoon sherry
2 minced onions
½ cup bread crumbs
2 tablespoons Parmesan cheese
1 teaspoon parsley
2 tablespoons oil

Select large, fresh mushrooms. Clean and remove stems. Saute stems in melted butter and sherry.

Stuff mushrooms with a mixture of minced onions, bread crumbs, Parmesan cheese, and sauteed stems. Then sprinkle with fresh parsley and oil. Bake 20 minutes at 350° or broil 5 minutes. Serves 3-4.

Simple Shrimp Dip

3 jars shrimp cocktail in tomato sauce
1 8-ounce package cream cheese

Remove shrimp from jars, reserving sauce. Cut shrimp in halves.

Whip cream cheese until soft and creamy. Blend in shrimp sauce. Pour in shrimp. Makes 2½ cups.

Serve with chips, bugles, or assorted crackers for a quick, unexpected hors d'oeuvre.

Calamari al Sugo di Lemone
(Squid Rings in Lemon Juice)

1 pound squid
Juice of two lemons
1 bud garlic
1 tablespoon olive oil
1 tablespoon parsley
Salt
Pepper

Clean the squid thoroughly, making sure all mucus lining is removed. Boil tentacles and body in salted water for 20 minutes. Drain and cut squid cylinder into rings.

Combine the lemon juice, garlic and other ingredients. Pour over squid. Let marinate 1 hour. Serves 6-8.

The tentacles and body of squid can combine to make an exotic appetizer. This conversational appetizer is a light tempter to any festive meal.

Marinated Artichokes

⅓ cup red wine
⅓ cup wine vinegar
¼ cup salad oil
1 small onion, sliced in rings
2 tablespoons fresh parsley
1 clove garlic, crushed
1 teaspoon salt
Dash ground pepper
1 tablespoon oregano
1 large can or package frozen artichokes
1 pound fresh mushrooms

In saucepan, combine first nine ingredients and bring to a boil. Add artichokes and mushrooms. Carrots and cauliflower may also be used.

Return mixture to boil and simmer uncovered for 10 minutes. Cool and chill in covered container for 24 hours before serving. Store in refrigerator up to 2 weeks. Serves 8-10.

Crabmeat Spread

1 large tin crabmeat or lobster (8 ounces)
1 large package cream cheese (8 ounces)
1 teaspoon grated onion
Few dashes Worchestershire sauce
Salt and pepper

Flake crabmeat; save juice and moisten cream cheese with it. Mix well all ingredients except the crabmeat, adding crabmeat last. Makes 2 cups.

Ricotta Dip

1 pound ricotta cheese
1 cup sour cream
1 small onion, grated
½ teaspoon thyme
½ teaspoon parsley
½ teaspoon rosemary
1 teaspoon lemon juice
Salt and pepper

Cream together ricotta cheese and sour cream. Add the remaining ingredients. Use for fresh vegetables. Refrigerate between servings. Makes 3 cups.

Chilled Clam Dip

1 can clams (7-ounce) with ¼ cup of its liquid
2 3-ounce packages cream cheese
2 teaspoons cut chives or green onion tops
¼ teaspoon salt
1 teaspoon Worcestershire sauce
3 drops tabasco sauce
1 tablespoon lemon juice
4-5 sprigs parsley

Combine ingredients and blend until smooth. Serve with toast squares or crackers. Makes about 1¾ cups.

Herring in Cocktail Tomatoes

Beautiful when alternated with spinach balls.

20 cocktail tomatoes
1 jar herring in sour cream (8 ounces)
4 ounces cream cheese

Core and clean cocktail tomatoes. Allow the herring in sour cream to soften. Chop the herring with a potato masher or food processor, but do not puree; leave herring in small bits. Add cream cheese which has already been creamed. Blend together. With a small spoon, drop the herring mixture into the tomatoes. Garnish with paprika. Serves 6-8.

Spinach Balls

These tangy hors d'oeuvres freeze very well. Reheat on foil.

1 package chopped spinach (10 ounce)
1 cup bread crumbs
3 eggs
6 tablespoons melted butter
¼ cup Parmesan cheese
¼ teaspoon thyme
Dash cayenne pepper
1 teaspoon Accent

Cook spinach; drain well. Mix bread crumbs, beaten eggs, butter, Parmesan cheese, thyme, pepper, and Accent with spinach. Shape into balls. Place on cookie sheet.

Bake 15 minutes at 350°. Makes approximately 30. The balls will puff. Serves 8.

Artichoke Spread

1 can artichokes (2 ounce)
1 cup Parmesan cheese
1 cup mayonnaise
Dash paprika

Cup up artichokes. Combine with cheese and mayonnaise. Place in ungreased baking dish. Sprinkle with paprika. Bake at 350° for 30 minutes. Spread on toast triangles or crackers. Serves 8-10.

Bacon Beauties

Wrap water chestnuts or shrimp in partially cooked bacon. Broil in oven. Keep piping hot in chafing dish.

Pecan Cheese Ball

¾ cup pecans
1 8-ounce package cream cheese
1 tablespoon A-1 steak sauce
1½ teaspoons chili powder

Chop pecans finely. Blend together cheese, A-1 sauce, and chili powder. Shape into a ball. Wrap in foil and chill until firm. Serves 6-8.

A light and tasty appetizer for any time of year, this is a must on Christmas Eve, for the traditional fish feast.

Hot Anchovy Dip

1 can anchovies (2 ounce)
1 stick butter or margarine (¼ pound)
1 teaspoon lemon juice
1 bunch celery

In warmer over candle, or in small saucepan on stove, dissolve anchovies in butter or margarine with lemon juice.

Clean and cut celery hearts into 4- to 5-inch sticks. Use some leaves of celery to decorate. Serves 6-8.

Salads

Cranberry Wreath

3 packages strawberry gelatin
2 cups boiling water
1 pound cranberries, cooked according to package directions for cranberry sauce
1 orange, peeled & cut
1 cup grapes
1 large can crushed pineapple
1 cup chopped nuts

Mix gelatin with water. When cool, add other ingredients. Pour into ring molds for seasonal shapes. Serves 12.

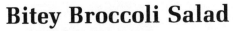

Bitey Broccoli Salad

1 pound fresh broccoli
1 small jar Spanish olives
Italian dressing

Boil broccoli just three minutes, add olives and toss with Italian dressing. Serves 4-6.

Lime-Pineapple Mousse

1 small can crushed pineapple
1 3-ounce package lime gelatin
2 tablespoons lemon juice
¼ teaspoon salt
1 can cold evaporated milk
½ cup chopped nuts
½ cup chopped celery

Add water to juice from pineapple to make 1¼ cups. Boil. Add to gelatin. Add salt and lemon juice, then chill until slightly thickened. Stir in milk, nuts, celery and reserved pineapple. Chill until firm. Serves 6-8.

A favorite for years at parties and Christmas buffets has been this very rich, red ring of cherry gelatin full of fruits and nuts and topped with whipped topping. Garnished with celery leaves and cherries, it is a beautiful wreath—a tasty, light balance to salty party hams.

Della Robbia Gelatin Ring

1 large package cherry gelatin
1 can pineapple chunks
1 apple
1 orange
¾ cup chopped walnuts
1 cup chopped, canned peaches
1 cup whipping cream or topping

Dissolve gelatin in 1 cup boiling water. Add 1 cup ice cubes. (This is 2 cups less water than indicated on the package.)

Add pineapple and its juice, apple (peeled and cubed), orange (peeled and cubed), walnuts, peaches or other desired fruit. Pour into large ring mold so that the mold is chock full of the fruits and nuts. Let jell. Unmold by setting the ring mold in warm water. Place "fruit wreath" on pedestal cake dish.

Decorate with whipped cream or whipped dairy product only on top, letting the bright red gelatin mold form the base of the wreath. Use celery leaves and cherries to complete the decoration and a Christmas Creation is ready! Serves 12.

The rich, heavy foods of the holidays often leave the stomach over-taxed. The tradition of a fresh fruit salad has a two-fold pleasure—it adds a delicate balance to the heavy foods of celebrations and it is a perfect complement to leftover turkey, ham, or beef.

"Day After the Feast" Fruit Salad

2 oranges
2 apples
1 grapefruit
2 bananas
½ pound seedless grapes
1 can chunk pineapple
1 can peaches
1 can or small bottle carbonated cherry soda
10-12 maraschino cherries

Clean and chunk all fresh fruits. We leave the peelings on apples if they are cut small enough. Combine fresh and canned fruits, including juice. Add cherry soda and garnish with maraschino cherries. Store in refrigerator. Use for two or three meals or a cheery breakfast/brunch. For added zing, use champagne instead of cherry soda. Serves 6-8.

Our Favorite Tossed Salad

Nothing accents red pastas and hearty red soups like a tart, fresh salad.

½ head iceberg lettuce
Romaine lettuce (1 bunch)
Tomatoes
1 stalk celery
Several black olives
2 radishes

Dressing:
¼ cup olive oil
⅓ cup vegetable oil
⅓ cup wine vinegar
Dash black pepper
Salt
1 clove garlic rubbed in bowl

When vegetables are at their tender peak, very few accents are needed. The subtle complement of olive oil, vegetable oil, and wine vinegar tossed gently over coarsely cut vegetables is a beautiful addition to any meal, and can be developed into a meal in itself.

We like the combination of firm head lettuce with crisp tender Romaine, torn by hand and dried gently. Use any combination of tomatoes, cucumbers, celery, broccoli, olives, carrots, and radishes with a light dressing. The salad should be well tossed, but not dripping in oil. Serves 6.

Fishes

Fish in Paper Pouches

4 filets halibut, whiting, or cod (2 pounds)
½ pound mushrooms, chopped
2 teaspoons parsley
Salt and pepper
4 tablespoons olive oil
4 teaspoons chopped prosciutto or spiced Canadian bacon
1 bay leaf, crumbled
4 teaspoons lemon juice

Cut aluminum foil or brown paper bag large enough to wrap each fish. Sprinkle each filet with ¼ of remaining ingredients. Wrap paper or foil around filet and put in baking dish. Bake at 350° for 25-30 minutes. Open "blanket" on dish. Serves 4.

Roman Snapper

½ cup butter
¼ cup lemon juice
dash Worcestershire sauce
4 red snapper fillets
1 cup crabmeat
¼ cup melted butter
1½ teaspoons butter
1½ teaspoon flour
½ cup half & half cream
½ teaspoon salt
dash white pepper
½ cup dry bread crumbs
8 green pepper strips

Combine butter, lemon juice, Worcestershire sauce in small saucepan. Cook over medium heat, stirring often, until heated. Place fillets in baking pan. Broil 10-15 minutes, basting with lemon butter. Saute crabmeat in ¼ cup butter, about 3 minutes; set aside. Melt remaining 1½ teaspoon butter in heavy saucepan. Add flour, stirring until smooth. Cook 1 minute stirring constantly. Gradually stir in half & half cream. Cook over medium heat until thick and bubbly. Add salt & pepper, and crabmeat on top of each fillet. Sprinkle bread crumbs over crabmeat. Garnish with green peppers. Bake at 350° ten minutes. Broil until bread crumbs are brown. Serves 4.

Christmas Eve Calamari (Squid)

2½ pounds squid
2 cups bread crumbs
½ cup Parmesan cheese
2 eggs
1 tablespoon parsley
1 teaspoon salt
Pepper
1 teaspoon garlic, minced

Buy fresh or frozen squid, preferably cleaned. If not cleaned, be sure to turn squid inside out, eliminating all mucus lining. Clean the cavity of the squid thoroughly. Scald squid for 1 minute moment in boiling water. Prepare the stuffing as follows. Soften the bread crumbs by soaking in cold water. Squeeze out all water. Add to the bread crumbs the Parmesan cheese, eggs, parsley, salt, pepper, and garlic. Mix the stuffing carefully and stuff the squid cavity.

Sauce:

1 onion, chopped
1 garlic clove, chopped
1 can tomatoes (1 pound)
1 can tomato paste (6 ounces)
Parmesan cheese

Make a tomato sauce made by browning the onion and garlic, adding tomatoes and tomato paste, and enough water to make a medium sauce. Simmer the sauce for 30 minutes.

Cover the squid with sauce. Sprinkle with Parmesan cheese and bake for 45 minutes at 350°.

Reserve the tentacles. Children love to look at them and gourmands will appreciate touching up a finished dish. The tentacles are also good as hors d'oeuvres, marinated in lemon juice. Serves 6-8.

White Fish in Red Sauce

Good with rice or fettucine with basil.

2-3 pounds fish (perch, cod, or turbot)
1 can tomatoes or 4 small tomatoes, peeled and cut
2 tablespoons butter
4 tablespoons Parmesan cheese

Grease a small baking dish. Add fish and tomatoes. Dot with butter and sprinkle with grated Parmesan cheese. Bake 30 minutes at 350°. Serves 4-6.

Italian Stuffed Trout

2-3 pounds fresh trout
Butter to taste
Salt
3 tablespoons butter
3-4 tablespoons celery, chopped
3-4 medium shrimp, chopped
1 small onion, chopped
1 cup bread crumbs
1 egg
1 tablespoon parsley
Pepper
Olive oil
Lemons

Choose a fresh trout. Have the fish cleaned by a butcher, leaving head on. Clean cavity of fish; line with butter and salt.

In 3 tablespoons butter, saute celery, shrimp, and onion. Soften bread crumbs in cold water; squeeze all water out. Add egg, parsley, salt, and pepper. Add sauteed shrimp and celery mixture. Mix thoroughly. Stuff fish and secure with toothpicks or thread. Brush fish with olive oil and bake for 1 hour at 350°. Garnish with lemons for an elegant entree. Serves 4-6.

Beautiful with shrimp tails artistically arranged in a copper dish. Elegant on a table!

Stuffed Shrimp in Sherry Sauce

2 pounds shrimp
Stuffing for Trout (see previous recipe)
Butter
½ cup sherry
Parsley

Clean 2 pounds boiled jumbo shrimp, leaving tails intact. Butter a casserole or copper dish for oven. Slit center of shrimp. (For smaller shrimp, the stuffing may be placed in the curvature of the shrimp.)

Prepare the stuffing for Italian Stuffed Trout. Stuff shrimp and place in baking dish.

Dot with butter, and add sherry. Bake 20 minutes at 350°. Garnish with parsley. Serves 4.

Broiled Scallops and Mushrooms

Low in calories and high in protein—festive for any occasion! Shrimp may be substituted for half the scallops.

2 pounds scallops
Flour to coat
1 pound fresh mushrooms
1 teaspoon parsley
Salt and pepper
6-7 tablespoons butter
4 tablespoons fine bread crumbs
Parsley

Clean fresh scallops. Dip each scallop in flour. Grease bottom of baking casserole or copper pan with butter. Clean and slice mushrooms. Place mushrooms and scallops into baking dish. Season with parsley, salt, and pepper to taste. Dot with butter. Broil gently for 5-10 minutes, turning often and watching closely as scallops brown quickly. Remove from broiler. Sprinkle enough bread crumbs over the top to cover. Return to broiler until golden brown. Garnish with parsley. Serves 4.

Poached Salmon with Holiday Sauce

7-8 pounds whole salmon

Sauce:

½ cup butter
3 tablespoons cornstarch
¼ teaspoon salt
1 tablespoon sugar
2 cups cream
2½ cups champagne
2 egg yolks

Poach salmon in large pan of salted water about one-half hour. Carefully lift salmon out of water and place on large platter.

Melt butter in sauce pan. Combine dry ingredients with cream until well blended. Add cream and dry ingredients slowly to warm butter, stirring constantly. Remove from heat. Add champagne. Beat egg yolks. Add gently to warm sauce. Spoon over salmon just before serving. Garnish platter with thin slices of lemon and oranges.

Baccala in Wine

3-4 pounds salted baccala (cod)
½ cup olive oil
1 cup white wine

Soak salted baccala in water for 2 days before using it. Brown each piece of fish in olive oil. Then place in fish poacher or narrow baking dish (approximately the size of a loaf bread pan). Cover with wine. Let poach in 350° oven 45 minutes. Remove to platter. Garnish with lemon wedges and parsley. Serves 6-8.

A Mediterranean favorite served in fine Roman restaurants as well as in the tappa bars of Spain.

Deep Fried Squid Rings

2½ pounds cleaned squid
2 eggs, well beaten
1 cup fine bread crumbs

Boil whole, cleaned squid in large kettle. Cool, and cut body of squid into 1-inch rings. Dip each ring in egg batter and then in bread crumbs. Fry in hot fat. Drain on paper towels. Serve with lemon wedges. Serves 6-8.

Crisp Italian Baked Fish

2 pounds fish of choice
½ cup olive oil
1 teaspoon lemon juice
1 tablespoon parsley
½ pound mushrooms
½ cup fine bread crumbs

Place fish in shallow baking dish. Pour olive oil over filets. Add lemon juice, parsley, and mushrooms. Top with fine Italian bread crumbs. Bake at 375° until crust is crisp and fish flakes easily, about 25 minutes. Serves 4.

Chestnut Filled Capon

2 fresh or frozen young capons

Meats

Dressing:
2 cups bread crumbs
2 eggs
½ cup chopped celery
½ cup chopped onions
1 cup chestnuts
1 teaspoon salt
Dash pepper
½ teaspoon basil
½ teaspoon rosemary
½ teaspoon thyme
½ teaspoon sage
3 tablespoons butter
½ cup white wine

Soften the bread crumbs by soaking in cold water. Squeeze out water. Mix bread with remaining ingredients. Spoon into cavities of capon. Secure with skewers or truss with needle and thread. Bake a 350° for 2-2½ hours, basting often with white wine and butter. Serves 4.

Helen's Saute Steak

4 tablespoons butter
2 pounds steak (eye of round), sliced thin
2 large onions, sliced thin
1 pound mushrooms, sliced
¾ cup red wine

Melt butter in a heavy skillet. Saute steak in butter, then remove steak to a warming platter. Brown onions and mushrooms in the same butter. Add wine and simmer for 10 minutes. Pour this mixture over warm steak and serve immediately.

Thin slices of steak may be cut when the meat is semi-frozen; or have the butcher do it.

Meatballs can be many sizes! Small cocktail meatballs are good for soups and appetizers. Patties are good fried for entrees. Golf ball size are a nice accent to spaghetti.

Melt-in-Your-Mouth Meatballs

2 **pounds lean ground chuck (or a combination of 1 pound chuck, ½ pound ground pork, and ½ pound ground veal)**
2 **cups Italian bread crumbs or hard bread**
4 **large eggs**
½ **cup Parmesan cheese**
1 **tablespoon parsley**
1 **clove garlic, minced (or 1 teaspoon garlic powder)**
1 **teaspoon salt**
Dash pepper
1 **small onion, minced**

Soak bread in cold water; squeeze out water. Combine all ingredients and mix well with hands. Form into balls of desired size.

Place meatballs on teflon-coated or lightly greased baking dishes. Brown in oven at 400° for about 15 minutes. Drain and freeze or simmer in spaghetti sauce. Serves 6-8.

Easy for large groups.

Fiesta Flank Steak

2 **pounds flank steak**
½ **cup red wine**
⅓ **cup olive oil**
¼ **cup wine vinegar**
1 **small onion, minced**
1 **carrot, chopped**
1 **clove garlic, minced**
1 **bay leaf**
1 **lemon peel**
1 **teaspoon oregano**
1 **teaspoon rosemary**
3 **tablespoons olive oil**
Salt and pepper

Marinate steak overnight in a mixture of the next 10 ingredients. Remove meat from marinade. Pat dry. Rub with 3 tablespoons olive oil, and season with salt and pepper. Place in roasting pan. Bake at high temperature (450°) 10-15 minutes depending on desired doneness. (Rare: 10 minutes. Medium: 15 minutes.) Steak should be sliced diagonally in narrow strips. Half of the marinade may be heated and poured over the cooked steak. Serves 4-6.

Italian Braised Beef

3-4 pounds rump roast or brisket
1 cup red wine
1 clove garlic
¼ cup chopped celery
1 teaspoon salt, pepper to taste
1 onion, chopped
1 carrot, cut up
1 teaspoon parsley
1 teaspoon lemon juice

Although beef has been a delicacy in parts of Italy, Italian treatment of beef in America can add fragrant variety to a meal. American meat, Italian flavor—elegant combination!

Marinate the roast for several hours in wine with garlic. Using wines judiciously can add delights to ordinary dishes, but overdone or misused wines can destroy pure flavors. And garlic, although a favorite spice of Italian cooking, should never be over-used.

After the meat is marinated, discard the clove of garlic and set the marinade aside temporarily. Dry the roast thoroughly, and dip in flour. Brown gently in bacon fat or oil.

Now the marinade and meat can be reunited in a Dutch oven or heavy pot. Water or stock should cover about half of the meat. Add the remaining ingredients. Simmer the roast at low heat until tender, approximately 3 hours. Serves 8-10.

Our Favorite Pork Spaghetti Sauce

Pastas

2-3 pounds pork ribs or chops
1 tablespoon oil
1 large onion, chopped
2 cloves garlic, minced
1 tablespoon parsley
1 teaspoon salt
½ teaspoon crushed red pepper
2 large cans ripe tomatoes
2 large cans tomato paste

Brown pork and onion in oil. Add remaining ingredients and enough water to make a thin sauce. Let simmer for 1½ hours; the sauce will thicken. Over spaghetti, this sauce serves 8.

Anchovy Spaghetti

¼ cup olive oil
¼ cup butter
3 cloves garlic, chopped
2 cans (2 ounces) anchovies
⅓ cup parsley
1½ pounds spaghetti of choice

Brown garlic in melted butter and olive oil. Add anchovies and parsley. Let anchovies dissolve. Boil spaghetti in salted water. Drain well. Pour sauce over spaghetti immediately. Serves 4-6.

Cannelloni

Shells:

5 eggs
1¼ cups flour
¼ teaspoon salt
1 teaspoon butter or margarine

Filling:

2 pounds ricotta cheese
⅓ cup grated Parmesan cheese
1 tablespoon chopped parsley
1 8-ounce package mozzarella cheese, diced
2 eggs
1 teaspoon salt
Basic tomato sauce (see page 24)
2 tablespoon Parmesan cheese

In a medium bowl, combine 5 eggs, 1¼ cups flour, ¼ teaspoon salt, and 1½ cups water. With electric mixer, beat until smooth. Melt 1 teaspoon butter in a 7" skillet. Pour in 2 tablespoons of batter and rotate pan quickly to spread batter evenly over bottom. Cook over medium heat until top of shell is dry, but do not brown the bottom. Turn out on a wire rack to cool.

Combine filling ingredients and beat with a wooden spoon until well blended. Place about ¼ cup of the filling in each shell and roll up. Spoon basic tomato sauce into a baking dish. Place filled shells, seam side down, in single layer, in dish. Cover with more sauce. Sprinkle with 2 tablespoons grated Parmesan cheese.

Bake uncovered 30 minutes at 350°, or until bubbly. Serves 10-12.

Homemade Noodles

3 cups all-purpose flour
½ teaspoon salt
3 eggs
Warm water (enough to make a stiff dough)

Quick freezing keeps cut noodles fresh! So simple, so efficient. . . and ready to be dropped, still frozen, into boiling water when needed.

Sift flour and salt together. Place in a large bowl, add eggs and enough water to make a stiff dough. Mix together well. Knead until smooth. Divide into four balls. Cover and let stand 10 minutes.

Roll out the pasta on a floured board to ⅛-inch thickness. Cut into ¼-inch-wide strips. Another way to cut the noodles is to roll the floured dough like a jelly roll, cut into segments of the desired width, unroll the noodles, and spread them on a tray.

To make noodles with the pasta machine—let the machine do the kneading by running the dough through the widest slot many times. Then put it through at decreasing sizes on the machine indicator until you reach the desired thickness (No. 1 or 2). Next, put on the noodle cutting attachment and presto—cut noodles.

Unless the noodles are to be used immediately, dry or quick freeze. I can nostalgically visualize my grandmother's kitchen with clean towels and noodles spread all over every flat surface and each hanging on the backs of chairs.

Not long ago, Mama Helen Fuscaldo devised a quick freeze method which will forever eliminate that image and that mess!

As soon as each batch is cut, we place the noodles on teflon cookie trays and run to the freezer. We quick freeze them before packing them in cardboard boxes for the final freezing.

Noodle varieties: The size the noodle is cut determines the type. Wide, ½-inch noodles are called fettuccine; broader (2-inch) noodles are good for Lasagna and Manicotti. Chopped spinach may be added to make green noodles. Serves 6-8.

Cream Crab Spaghetti

1 pound fettucini
3 tablespoons butter
6 ounces crabmeat
1 cup heavy cream
¼ cup Parmesan cheese

Cook fettucini in 3 quarts boiling, salted water for 10 minutes. Drain and reserve pasta. Melt butter in a skillet and add crabmeat, cream, and fettucini. Cook at medium heat for 5 minutes, or until thick. Stir in cheese. Serves 2-4.

Great for the rushed gourmet who doesn't have time to make pasta from scratch.

Stuffed Jumbo Shells

1 pound jumbo size sea shell macaroni
2 pounds ricotta cheese
2 tablespoons parsley
4 tablespoons grated Parmesan cheese
3 eggs

Boil macaroni in salted water until tender, approximately 15 minutes. Drain and rinse with cold water, making sure the shells are separated. Combine cheeses, parsley, and eggs. Spoon into shells. Arrange in casserole. Top with pork spaghetti sauce (see recipe on page 19). Bake 20 minutes at 350°. Serves 8.

Freezes well.

Manicotti with Spinach

½ pound manicotti shells
1 pound fresh spinach
2 tablespoons butter
2 eggs
1 pound ricotta cheese
½ cup Parmesan cheese

Boil manicotti shells in salted water until tender, approximately 15 minutes. Drain and separate on waxed paper. Cook spinach until tender but still bright green; add butter while warm. Mix eggs, cheeses, and spinach. Spoon into shells. Arrange in casserole. Top with pork spaghetti sauce (see recipe on page 19). Bake at 350° for 20 minutes. Serves 4.

White Clam Sauce

½ cup olive oil
4 tablespoons butter
1 clove garlic, minced
3-7½-ounce cans clams
1 teaspoon salt
½ cup parsley
Pepper to taste
1 pound pasta

Heat olive oil, butter, and garlic until garlic is tender. Add clams and clam liquid. Mix well. Add salt, parsley, and pepper and bring to a boil. Remove from heat. Pour sauce over cooked, drained pasta and serve immediately. Serves 4.

Shrimp Spaghetti

Canned clams or crabmeat may be used instead of shrimp.

1 onion
1 clove garlic, minced
3 tablespoons olive oil
2 cans tomatoes (16 ounce can) or 8 whole tomatoes
1 6-ounce can tomato paste
1 tablespoon salt
1 teaspoon red pepper, crushed
1 teaspoon parsley
1 pound shrimp, cut up
1 cup wine
Spaghetti

Brown onion and garlic in olive oil. Add tomatoes, tomato paste, and enough water to make a sauce. Season with salt, pepper, and parsley. Let sauce simmer 1 hour. Cook shrimp in wine. Add wine and shrimp to sauce and cook 10 minutes. Served over boiled spaghetti. Serves 6-8.

Ravioli

Slightly browned meatballs also make a delicious filling. Chopped spinach and Parmesan cheese make another variation.

Pasta dough:
3 cups flour
¼ teaspoon salt
2 eggs
2 tablespoons butter
1 cup warm water

Sift flour and salt together. Place on a board. Drop eggs in center; add butter. Mix gradually. Add enough water to make a rather stiff dough. Knead until smooth. Cover and let stand 10 minutes. Cut in half, and roll each half until very thin.

Filling:

2 pounds ricotta cheese
2 eggs
1 teaspoon salt
1 tablespoon parsley
3 tablespoons grated Parmesan cheese

Mix ingredients with fork. Drop by spoonfuls on floured dough. Small muffin-like tins work very well to place dough and filling. Then place second layer of dough on top. Prick and cut squares of ravioli. Mama Helen Fuscaldo suggests quick freezing ravioli on teflon trays, then boxing the delicacies in layered freezer boxes. If the ravioli are not frozen, they must be dried before boiling in salted water. Boil small portions at a time, and drain gently. Serves 8-10.

Basic Tomato Sauce

1 small onion, chopped
1 clove garlic, minced
3 tablespoons olive oil or vegetable oil
1 can whole tomatoes (1 pound) or 4 fresh tomatoes, pared
2 6-ounce cans tomato paste
1 teaspoon salt
Dash crushed red pepper
1 tablespoon parsley
Approximately 1 quart water

Brown onion and garlic in oil. Crush or smash tomatoes with fork or potato masher. Add tomatoes and their juice. Empty tomato paste into sauce, and fill cans with warm water to remove any paste left in bottom. Add seasonings and enough water to make a thin sauce. Let simmer for 45 minutes to 1 hour, or until as thick as desired. Approximately 1 quart sauce.

Lasagna—easy enough for our youngest son to make, and good enough for any occasion!

Light Lasagna

1 pound lasagna noodles
1 pound ricotta cheese
¼ cup Parmesan cheese
1 pound mozarella cheese
Pork Spaghetti Sauce (see recipe on page 19)

Boil lasagna noodles 20 minutes or until tender. Drain and separate on waxed paper. In a baking dish, alternate layers of noodles with ricotta cheese, grated Parmesan cheese, and spaghetti sauce. Top with strips of mozzarella cheese. Cover pan with aluminum foil. Bake 40 minutes at 350°.

An especially good complement to fish.

Basil Fettucini

1 pound fettuccine
2 tablespoons butter
2 cloves garlic
½ cup olive oil
3 tablespoons basil leaves
½ cup grated Parmesan cheese

Boil fettuccine in salted water. Drain. Sprinkle butter over noodles. Prepare a paste of garlic, olive oil, basil leaves, and grated Parmesan cheese. Pour over fettuccine and serve immediately. Serves 4.

Baked Zucchini Tiela

6-8 zucchini, cleaned and sliced
8 potatoes, peeled and sliced
4 green peppers, sliced
2 1-pound cans tomatoes
Butter
6 tablespoons Parmesan cheese

Grease a baking dish. Alternate zucchini, potaotes, peppers, and tomatoes. Dot with butter and sprinkle with Parmesan cheese. Bake at 350° for approximately 1 hour, or until vegetables are tender. Serves 8.

Green Beans al Italiana

2 pounds fresh green beans
1 small ham bone or ½ pound salt pork

Dressing:

½ medium onion, minced
½ cup olive oil
1 tablespoon vinegar

Clean and string green beans. Bring to boil in 2 quarts water with ham bone or salt pork. Cook until tender. Drain water. Add dressing, toss, and serve hot or cold. Serves 8-10.

Baked Zucchini Boats

6 medium sized zucchini
6 tablespoons butter
6 tablespoons Parmesan cheese

Boil zucchini until tender but not mushy. Drain. Rinse with cool water. Slit zucchini lengthwise. Arrange in shallow greased baking dish. With sharp knife, cut criss-cross slits in zucchini. Insert butter in slits and sprinkle with Parmesan cheese. Place under broiler until golden brown. Serve hot. Serves 6.

Baked Zucchini

6 medium zucchini
6 tablespoons Parmesan cheese
1 28-ounce can tomatoes
Butter
Toasted bread crumbs

Grease a small casserole. Peel and clean zucchini. Cut into slices. Place half the sliced zucchini in casserole. Sprinkle with 3 tablespoons grated Parmesan cheese. Layer half the tomatoes, remaining zucchini, cheese, and tomatoes. Dot with butter and spinkle with toasted bread crumbs. Bake 1 hour at 350°. Serves 6-8.

Tomatoes Stuffed with Spinach

6 medium sized tomatoes
6 teaspoons butter
2 pounds fresh spinach
6 tablespoons Parmesan cheese

Wash and core tomatoes. Scoop out most but not all of the pulp. Put 1 teaspoon butter in the bottom of each tomato. Drop spinach in boiling salted water. Boil just one minute. Chop coarsely. Fill tomato-cavities with spinach. Sprinkle each tomato with a tablespoon of Parmesan cheese. Place tomatoes in buttered casserole. Bake at 350° 1 hour or until tomatoes are tender. Serves 6.

Pita Piata

2 cups white wine
1 cup salad oil
½ cup shortening
6 eggs
4 tablespoons granulated sugar
8 cups sifted flour (sift before measuring)
1 jigger whiskey (2 tablespoons)
3 boxes (15-ounce size) white raisins
10 cups chopped walnuts
Dash cinnamon
½ cup light brown sugar, packed
1 jar (24 ounces) honey
½ cup honey for brushing

Desserts & Party Foods

This very traditional Calabrion Italian glazed Nut Roll is delicious with party drinks or coffee

Boil first three ingredients for ½ minute. Set aside to cool. Beat eggs very well. Add granulated sugar to eggs and mix. Add egg mixture to cooled wine/oil mixture. Pour this over flour in large mixing bowl. Mix well. It should be the consistency of a soft dough.

Divide the dough into six balls and replace in bowl. Set aside in refrigerator while you mix the whiskey, raisins, nuts, cinnamon, brown sugar, and jar of honey.

Roll each ball of dough as thin as piecrust, about ¼ inch thick, into a rectangle approximately 12" X 16". Spread 1/6 of the raisin and nut mixture on each. Roll up lengthwise, like a jelly roll. Prick ends closed. Shape into wreaths or candy canes.

Bake on greased cookie sheets about 1½ hours at 300°. Brush with honey for the last 20 minutes of baking.

Makes 6 wreaths or canes, 10 servings each.

This versatile dough is simple enough for children to make. Deep fried, it is at its best. On Christmas Eve, small sardines are traditionally placed in the dough before it is deep fried.
Wreath-shaped frittas, freshly fried, are a perfect companion for the assortment of fishes at that celebration.

Fritta

2 packages of active dry yeast
2½ cups warm water
½ cup milk
1 teaspoon salt
½ cup margarine
½ cup sugar
2 eggs
9 cups flour

The basic fritta dough can be baked or fried. It is good for pizza, pepperoni and fish rolls, and for doughnut-like pastries. Dissolve yeast in warm water and add the other ingredients. Mix well. Let the dough rise once.

For Pizza:

After the dough has risen once, shape on greased pizza pan. Let rise again before adding toppings. Bake pizza 20 minutes at 425°.

For Baked Rolls:

After the dough has risen once, shape into small (2-inch) balls and let rise again. Bake 20 minutes at 400°.

For Deep Fried Breads:

After the dough has risen once, cut a 2-inch chunk of dough with kitchen shears, then press finger through center, making a doughnut-shaped pastry. Let rise about 10 minutes more. Drop into deep fat. Turn when golden brown, and continue frying. Drain on paper towels.

Variations:

Sprinkle sugar on dessert frittas while still warm. This traditional Christmas Eve pastry is still good on Christmas morning.

Egg whites brushed on baked frittas give a golden glaze.

Try filling the rolls with anchovies, sardines, pepperoni, asparagus, or cream cheese.

For Pepperoni Rolls:

After the dough has risen once, cut a 3 inch portion of dough with kitchen shears. Flatten each piece wih palm of hand. Lay two pieces of pepperoni on flattened dough and roll as for jelly roll. Press ends of roll together and let raise a second time on greased cookie sheet. If rolls tend to separate, press ends together before baking. Bake until golden brown at 350°. Brush baked rolls with beaten egg for a glossy appearance.

Lemon Fruit Cake

1 pound whole pecans
1 pound candied cherries (leave whole)
1 pound white raisins
4 cups sifted flour
1 teaspoon baking powder
1 teaspoon salt
1 pound butter or margarine
2 cups sugar
6 eggs
1 ounce lemon extract

Dredge the nuts, raisins, and cherries in a small amount of the flour. Set aside. Sift the balance of the flour with the baking powder and salt. Set aside.

Soften the butter and put in a large mixing bowl. Add sugar a little at a time; cream well. Add eggs one at a time, beating well after each addition. Add the flour mixture a little at a time. Then add the nut mixture alternately with the lemon extract.

Pour batter into a stem pan lined with brown paper and greased well. Bake at 300° for 2 hours, then at 325° for another hour, over a pan of hot water.

Wrap in plastic wrap while stil hot. Freeze or place a wine soaked cloth over cake. This procedure keeps fruit cake moist and flavorful.

Sunday Night Scones

6 cups all-purpose flour
¾ cup sugar
¾ cup butter or margarine
5 eggs
3 teaspoons baking powder
¾ cup milk

Mix flour and sugar. Work in the butter. Beat 4 eggs with the baking powder and milk, then stir into the flour mixture. Mix well. On a floured board, roll out to about 1 inch thick. Cut into rounds. Place on greased baking sheet. Brush the tops with the remaining egg, well beaten. Bake 15 minutes at 400°. Makes 2 dozen.

For Sunday night tea—fresh preserves, cheeses, a pot of hot tea, and it's time to celebrate!

Orange Snowballs

½ cup melted butter
1 cup powdered sugar
¼ cup frozen orange juice concentrate
2¾ cup vanilla wafer crumbs
1 cup chopped nuts
Coconut, shredded

Butter icing:

Mix 2 tablespoons butter with 1 cup powdered sugar.

Mix melted butter, powdered sugar, orange juice concentrate, vanilla wafer crumbs, and chopped nuts. Shape into small balls, dip in butter icing, and toss in coconut. Store refrigerated in an airtight container.

Italian Bowknots

6 eggs
3 tablespoons granulated sugar
¼ teaspoon salt
½ teaspoon orange flavoring
1 teaspoon almond flavoring
3 cups flour
2 tablespoons butter
½ cup powdered sugar

Beat eggs lightly. Add granulated sugar, salt, and flavorings; blend thoroughly. Place flour on board and cut in butter. Add egg mixture and knead until a smooth ball is formed. If the dough is too soft, add a little flour, to make a firm, but not hard, dough. Set aside for 30 minutes. Then cut into 4 pieces. Roll on a well floured board until wafer thin. Cut with a pastry cutter into strips 6 inches long by ¾ inch wide. Pinch in center to form individual bowknots.

Fry bowknots about 3 minutes, or until light brown, in deep fat. Drain on paper towels. Sprinkle with powdered sugar (a flour sifter works very well) or, for variety, dip into warm honey. This delicate pastry may be stored in airtight containers in a cool room or frozen before festive occasions.

Piled deeply on bright platters, bowknots are the focal point of any party table. Makes about 5 dozen.

Pizzelle

Add your own favorite flavor, chocolate, anise, rum.

12 eggs
3½ cups sugar
2 cups oil
1 ounce lemon extract
1 ounce orange extract
1 teaspoon vanilla extract
6 cups flour
¼ teaspoon salt

Beat eggs well; add sugar gradually. Add oil and extracts; beat until blended. Sift the flour and salt together; add it to the mixture a little at a time.

Chill dough at least 2 hours. Chilling overnight or several days under refrigeration enhances flavor. Pour batter sparingly on pizzelle iron. Cook 2-3 minutes or until done. Makes 10 dozen.

Most new waffle irons today have pizzelle grills.

Tordillia (Italian Cookies)

1 cup red wine
1 cup oil
½ teaspoon cinnamon
½ teaspoon baking powder
1 teaspoon salt
Enough flour to make a soft dough
Honey

Mix first six ingredients; roll out ½ inch thick. My aunt uses her fingers to measure. Aunt Rosie adds, "Cut the strips one inch wide."

Cut each strip into 1-inch slices. Roll and form into small balls.

Grease a cookie sheet. Lay the finger-formed balls on the sheet. Slide a few at a time gently from the cookie sheet into deep fat. Fry until golden brown. Drain well. Place in a bowl and pour honey over cookies. Makes several dozen.

Store in tins or freeze.

Italian Butter Cookies

2 sticks butter
2 cups sugar
6 eggs
3 teaspoons vanilla
7 cups flour
2 tablespoons baking powder

Cream butter and sugar well. Add eggs and beat until creamy. Add vanilla and beat. Add flour and baking powder and mix well with hands until dough is stiff and dry, using a little more flour if needed. Refrigerate for several hours or overnight.

Break off pieces the size of a walnut and roll out about the thickness of a pencil. Form into a double strand and make into a small wreath. Bake 12-15 minutes at 375°. Makes about 7 dozen cookies.

Icing:

1 cup confectioner's sugar
1 tablespoon milk
1 teaspoon lemon extract

Combine icing ingredients and mix until smooth. Dip cookies in icing, or brush on with a pastry brush.

Store in tins or jars for the delight of young visitors at Christmas.

Christmas Caramel Corn

1 cup butter or margarine
2 cups brown sugar
½ cup corn syrup
1½ teaspoon salt
½ teaspoon baking soda
1½ teaspoons vanilla
24 cups popped popcorn

Gently melt butter; add brown sugar, corn syrup, and salt. Bring to a full boil, stirring. Let bubble for 5 minutes. Remove from heat; stir in soda and vanilla. Pour over popcorn, mixing well. Pour the mixture into a buttered 9" x 12" baking pan. Bake at 225° for 1½ hours, stirring every half hour. Cool; break apart and wrap.

Molded Strawberries

2 packages strawberry gelatin
1 can Eagle brand milk
17-ounce package flaked coconut
Coconut for coating
Green gum mints or candied cherries

Mix gelatin, milk, and coconut well; let stand overnight in refrigerator. Shape into strawberries and toss in grated coconut. Place on a plate or tray and keep refrigerated. Leaves can be made from strips of green gum mints or green candied cherries.

These add a beautiful touch of color to a simple platter. A plain tray of cookies becomes a proud part of the tea table with these strawberries.

New Year's Trifle

Lady fingers or sponge cake
Sherry
Vanilla custard or 2 packages vanilla pudding
2 boxes red gelatin
Bananas
Fresh strawberries or raspberries

Line a clear, 2-quart bowl with a double row of lady fingers or stale yellow sponge cake. Soak the cake or fingers in sherry, 1 tablespoon for every two lady fingers.

Prepare your favorite vanilla custard, or prepare 2 boxes vanilla pudding, reducing the milk in each by ½ cup.

Prepare 2 boxes red gelatin, using 1 cup less water than indicated on package. Chill.

Spread cooled custard or pudding on lady fingers. Top with bananas and berries. Add the chilled gelatin, and follow with another layer of bananas and berries.

"Trifle" is hardly the word for this mountain of rich creams, sherried cake, and fruited gelatins. Served in an antique or crystal glass bowl, it is a festive finale to any meal. Place it on the coffee table after a holiday meal; have a large spoon and some colorful bowls nearby, and you have an after-meal ceremony. On New Year's Day candy confetti and angelica can dress it up for the celebration.

Whipped Topping:

2 pints whipping cream
4 tablespoons sugar
1 teaspoon vanilla

Prepare whipped topping and mound on top of trifle. Garnish with more fruit, candy confetti, or angelica. Serves 8.

Variations: In place of sherry, use Amaretta di Saronno. Use cling peaches and almonds in place of strawberries and bananas. This variation adds an Italian touch to the holiday dessert.

Sour Cream Sugar Cookies

¾ cup butter
2 cups sugar
3 eggs
1 cup sour cream
1 teaspoon vanilla
2 teaspoons baking powder
2 teaspoons soda
6 cups flour

Cream butter and sugar. Beat eggs, and add alternately with sour cream. Add vanilla; mix well. Sift baking powder, soda, and flour together. Blend all ingredients.

Shape into Christmas or Chanukkah symbols. Bake 15 minutes at 425°, or until golden brown. Yields 6 dozen.

Stuffed Dates

Dates
Pecan halves
Powdered sugar

Slit fresh dates and remove the pits. Replace the pit with a pecan half. Sprinkle with powdered sugar.
Stuffed dates add a nice touch to a cookie tray!

Store in a box or cookie tin lined with waxed paper. Waxed paper between layers also helps the candy to store well.

Cubaita (Italian Almond Brittle)

2 pounds shelled almonds
2 orange peels, chopped fine
1 tangerine peel, chopped fine
1½ teaspoons cinnamon
1½ pounds sugar
12 ounces honey

Toast and coarsely chop the almonds. Add the peels and cinnamon. Set aside. Melt sugar in a large frying pan until light brown. Add honey and stir quickly. Add cinnamon and the almond mixture. Mix well. Pour on a board that has been wet with cold water. Spread the candy mixture out and let cool. Cut in bite-size pieces. Makes 3 pounds.

Anginettes

1 **cup butter**
1 **cup sugar**
4 **large eggs**
1 **cup orange juice**
1 **teaspoon orange extract**
1 **teaspoon lemon extract**
2 **tablespoons baking powder**
1 **teaspoon baking soda**
6 **cups flour**

Combine butter, sugar, and eggs; beat until light and fluffy. Add remaining ingredients except flour, which is added one cup at a time. Dough must be soft. Drop by teaspoonfuls on greased cookie sheet. Bake 12 minutes at 425°. Makes about 6 dozen cookies.

Amaretto Chestnuts

Better than after-dinner mints!

Chestnuts
Amaretto

Peel chestnuts and boil until crisp tender. Put chestnuts in container and cover with Amaretto. Let soak at least a week in refrigerator before serving.

Amaretti Cookies

1 **pound shelled almonds**
2 **cups confectioner's sugar**
2 **teaspoons vanilla**
½ **teaspoon almond extract**
2 **egg whites**

Grind almonds in electric blender until very fine. Put in small bowl. Add sugar, vanilla, and extract. Work with fingers until well blended. Stir in unbeaten egg whites. The dough will be sticky. Drop by teaspoonfuls on greased cookie sheet and bake 15-20 minutes, or until light brown, at 350°. Makes 2 dozen.

Toasted Cinnamon Pecans

1 pound pecan halves
2 tablespoons butter
2 egg whites
1 cup sugar
½ teaspoon cinnamon

Brown pecan halves in butter at 250° for 15 minutes. Cool and fold into two beaten egg whites, sugar, and cinnamon. Drop onto brown paper and bake 40 minutes at 275°. Watch closely. After completely cool, store in airtight container. Makes 1 pound pecans.

Spingie (New Year's Doughnuts)

2 cakes of fresh yeast
½ cup warm milk
2 cups flour
1 teaspoon salt
2 eggs

Soften yeast in warm milk; add remaining ingredients. Mix well. Let rise for 1 hour. Drop by spoonfuls into deep fat; fry until golden brown. Drain on paper towel. Dip in confectioner's sugar. Yields 2 dozen.

Glazed Nuts

1 cup sugar
½ cup water
¾ teaspoon salt
1 teaspoon vanilla
1 teaspoon cinnamon
1 pound nuts

Combine all ingredients except nuts. Simmer in thick-bottomed pan until syrup spins a small thread. Do not over-cook.

Remove from heat. Add nuts and stir thoroughly until syrup is crystalized. Turn out on a board and separate. Makes 1 pound nuts

Santa's Popcorn Balls

2 cups sugar
1 cup light corn syrup
1 cup water
3 tablespoons butter
2 quarts popped popcorn

Pour first four ingredients into heavy-bottomed pan. Cook, stirring often, until the syrup reaches the soft crack stage. Pour immediately over the popcorn. With rubber gloves or plastic bags on your hands, form into firm balls. Wrap in pretty cellophane or plastic wrap. Makes about 8 balls.

Display these popcorn balls in a large basket with a red ribbon tied on top—or in a clear crystal bowl.

Our children love making and sharing popcorn balls with friends. In our home, while the pita piatas were being formed on Christmas Eve, two of Santa's helpers, in the familiar form of two aunts, prepared Santa's Popcorn Balls. As our children became aware of the origin of some of the traditional Christmas rituals, they asked how popcorn balls became a part of an Italian-American Christmas celebration. The answer: "They fit in just as the two American aunts fit into the clan." And so our Christmas was enriched.

The cookies, red and green, look lovely combined in a serving dish.

Christmas Butter Balls

2 cups flour
¼ teaspoon salt
¾ cup butter or margarine
¼ cup sugar
1 cup nuts
1 teaspoon vanilla
Red and green food coloring (optional)
Powdered sugar

Sift flour; add salt, measure, and sift again. Cream butter thoroughly. Add sugar to butter; blend well. Add flour mixture. Mix well. Add nuts and vanilla. Divide dough into two parts.

To add color for the holiday season, blend a few drops of food coloring into each part of the dough.

Roll batter into walnut-sized balls and dip each ball in powdered sugar. Place cookies close together on a greased cookie sheet. Bake 10-15 minutes at 350°, or until lightly browned on bottom. When cool, roll the cookies in powdered sugar again. Makes 4 dozen.

Beverages

Sparkling Cranberry Punch

1 quart cranberry juice
¾ cup orange juice
½ cup lemon juice
2 teaspoons almond extract
1 28-ounce bottle ginger ale

Mix juices. Add almond extract and ginger ale.
Keep this punch cool with an elegant ice mold of cherries, orange slices, and mint leaves. To keep the fruit in a pretty design at the top of the ice ring, place the fruit in the bottom of a ring mold, add only ½ inch of water, and freeze. Add another inch; freeze. Then fill mold to the top and freeze.

Spiced After Dinner Coffee

8 cups Italian expresso coffee (brewed)
½ cup sugar
2 teaspoons whole cloves
5 sticks cinnamon
2 orange rinds
⅔ cup Amaretto
Whipped cream

Brew coffee to desired strength. In a saucepan, combine coffee, sugar, cloves, and cinnamon. Heat for 10 minutes, never allowing it to boil. Decorate cups with orange rind and pour in coffee. Add Amaretto and whipped cream.

Sangria for Holidays

A must with Festive Paella.

½ gallon red wine
Juice of 3 oranges
Juice of 2 lemons
1 cup sugar
1 lemon, sliced thinly
1 orange, sliced thinly

Mix all ingredients and refrigerate, preferably for 24 hours. Gin may be added for extra zing.

Frothy Eggnog for Fifteen

A mountain of chilled foam!

12 egg whites
4 cups whipping cream
12 egg yolks
3 cups half and half cream
1½ cups sugar
1 teaspoon vanilla
Dash nutmeg
3 cups bourbon (optional)

This lovely, frothy eggnog can be accomplished only by beating beating, beating!

Beat the egg whites and the whipping cream separately, both until stiff. Beat the egg yolks with the half and half, sugar, and vanilla. Combine with egg whites and whipping cream. Sprinkle nutmeg on top. If desired, spike the eggnog with 3 cups bourbon.

Christmas Champagne Punch

2 bottles white champagne
2 bottles white sauterne
1 bottle ginger ale

Combine; serve immediately.
Do not use an ice mold with this punch. Too much melted water will ruin the strength.

A rich topping for holiday coffees – My dad's specialty to the neighbors.

Coffee with Frothy Egg

1 cup coffee (brewed)
1 egg yolk
4 tablespoons sugar

Beat egg yolks with sugar until fluffy. Spoon into cups of hot coffee. Lovely holiday topper!

Coffee and Christmas pastries, a warm ending to the day.

Spring

"Natale con i Tuoi e Pasque Doui Vuoi"—"Christmas with your family and Easter wherever you want!"

So the old Italian proverb tells us, and so it is. The open road often entices us at Easter. Balmy air and the bright sun are indeed compelling, but no more compelling than the need to be bound in some way with family and close friends at this and every holiday.

The most poignant feelings emerge at these times; and the deeper the sentiment, the closer the nucleus of people with whom one wishes to share it.

When the physical presence of people we love is not possible, some bond is necessary to tie us to one another. Symbols and ritual do this. Food, at holiday celebrations, is one of the most pleasant of these symbols.

It is more than just tradition or habit—the food itself becomes the mortar, the link. The bond of support is food—either shared or withheld, in common consent.

Meatless meals for Christians during Lent and unleavened breads at Passover for Jews represent a sharing of pain and death, through withholding of succulent foods. All binding acts of a people together deepen their ties of understanding and loyalty to the cult or clan.

The bitter herbs and unleavened breads are soon replaced by tender early vegetables and golden mellow breads for spring celebrations.

The lamb, symbol for both Jewish and Christian celebrations, is particularly enjoyable in the spring.

At Easter as well as at the height of Passover, the lamb is the succulent and tasty climax of the feast. Even eaten alone, the lamb is a binding reminder of the lambs shared and sacrificed at man's earliest communal celebrations. Lamb—marinated, roasted, decorated, and delicately accompanied by mint and herb sauces—provides a tender nutrient in the spring.

Young capons, tasty chickens, cornish hens, succulent piglets, and decorated hams—all are found on the festive tables at this time. Creative new cakes, coconut-covered and lamb-shaped, are displayed along with tempting candies and fruited sweets, all fill the baskets and tables.

And finally, the egg, boiled and colored or placed in yellow, life-giving breads, adds to the symbols of life renewed, life nourished. Spring with all its joys is shared with family and friends—at home or wherever you want!

Antipasto

½ pound sliced prosciutto or cured ham (salami or capicollo)
¼ pound sliced mozzarella, provolone, swiss or fontina cheese
½ cup olive oil
⅓ cup wine vinegar
1 teaspoon lemon juice
1 bottle of Italian black olives (7 to 9 ounces)
1 bottle of capers (3 ounces)
1 bottle of vinegar peppers (8 ounces)
1 bottle of delicatessen onions (8 ounces)
1 jar marinated mushrooms (5½ ounces)
6 pieces of celery, washed and diced
1 can of anchovy fillets (1½ to 1¾ ounces) drained well (optional)
1 jar marinated artichoke hearts (6 ounces)
1 jar eggplants in oil (8 ounces)
2 to 3 pounds of shrimp which are boiled and cleaned
lettuce leaves to garnish

The beautiful variety of vegetables known as the antipasto is really a versatile meal in itself. With a loaf of crusty Italian bread, a balance of hams, cheese and little fishes, it is a celebration of color and cleverness.

Mix in a very large and deep bowl. Add oregano, garlic powder, olive oil and a touch of wine vinegar, and a little bit of lemon. Salt and pepper to taste.

Marinate about 1 hour prior to serving. Arrange on bed of lettuce, arranging in rows of meats, cheese and vegetables or combined together. Serves 8.

Variations

Use favorite festive platter, create rows or circles of green peppers, cherry tomatoes, celery hearts, wedges of mild but firm provolone cheese, or Greek feta cheese, salami or prosciutto, radish rosettes, and cucumber julliened, dark black olives or crushed green ones. A favorite part of the antipasto for us are the spicy black olives, seasoned with crushed red peppers. Pigs feet for the exotic and sardines and anchovies for the fish lovers go well.

For everyone who combines these beautiful fresh entrees, the fortified feast is fit for a king.

Brunch Prunes and Bacon

1 pound large pitted prunes
1 pound cheddar cheese, cut into 3/4-inch cubes
1 pound sliced bacon

Stuff prunes with cheese cubes. Wrap each with ½ slice bacon and secure with toothpick. Broil until bacon is crisp. Serve hot for brunch or party. Serves 10-12.

Caponata alla Siciliana

(Eggplant Marinade)

2 medium eggplants (cut into 1-inch cubes)
½ cup olive oil
2 onions, sliced
1 can tomatoes (16 ounces), chopped with liquid
1 cup diced celery or mushrooms
½ cup sliced pimiento stuffed olives
1 can (2½ ounces) sliced ripe olives
2 tablespoons capers
1 tablespoon pine nuts
3 tablespoons sugar
½ cup wine vinegar
Salt and pepper

In large skillet, saute eggplant in very hot olive oil about 10 minutes or until soft and slightly brown. Transfer eggplant with slotted spoon to large saucepan. Reduce heat under skillet and saute onions about 3 minutes, adding a little oil if necessary. When onions are golden brown, add tomatoes and celery. Simmer about 15 minutes or until celery is tender. Add olives, capers, and pine nuts.

Dissolve sugar in vinegar in small saucepan. Add salt and pepper and heat slightly. Stir into eggplant. Cover and simmer 30 minutes, stirring occasionally to distribute flavor evenly. Remove from heat; cool. Chill covered overnight. Serve at room temperature. Super with crackers or crusty bread. Caponata can also be frozen. Serves 8.

Melon and Prosciutto

A tasty tradition in Rome on Easter morning: the simple combination of honeydew or cantaloupe melon with dark rich red prosciutto.

Prosciutto is a highly spiced Italian (Parma) ham. Wrapped around a slice of cool sweet melon, the two combine to make a lovely appetizer or a light party hors d'oeuvre.

In America, prosciutto can be obtained in the deli section of supermarkets. (Canadian bacon can be substituted.) The thin ham is wrapped around bite-size pieces of melon, then secured with a toothpick. Simple—but superb!

Chicken Livers and Toast Triangles

¼ cup oil
1 pound chicken livers, finely chopped
¼ cup chopped onions
1 tablespoon minced fresh basil
Toast points
Salt and pepper

Heat oil. Add liver, onions and basil. Cook 10 min. Top toast with hot liver. Sprinkle with salt and pepper and serve hot. Serves 6-8.

Sizzling Mushrooms in Olive Oil

This delicate but simple food is a favorite in the tapa bars along the Mediterranean.

1 pound large fresh mushrooms
½ cup olive oil
Chopped prosciutto (optional)

Clean and dry mushrooms; remove stems. Heat oil in shallow skillet. Gently drop in caps and cook until golden brown.

A variation is to stuff caps with prosciutto. Drizzle with olive oil and put under broiler until brown, watching very closely so as not to burn the delicacies. Serves 4.

Steak with Fresh Mint

Fowl & Spring Meats

Flour
Salt and pepper
Oil
3 pounds round steak, cut in serving pieces
1 clove garlic
5 or 6 fresh mint leaves

Mix flour with salt and pepper; dredge steak. Heat oil; add garlic and mint leaves and saute a moment. Add steak and brown gently. Discard garlic and drain oil. Add enough water to cover steak. Simmer 20 minutes until tender. Place on hot platter. Garnish with mint sprigs. Serves 6.

Orange and Sherry Chicken Breasts

6 whole chicken breasts
1 teaspoon salt
2 cups sliced fresh mushrooms
1 large onion, sliced
1 large green pepper, slivered
1 cup orange juice
¼ cup dry sherry
½ cup water
1 tablespoon brown sugar
1 teaspoon salt
¼ teaspoon pepper
1 teaspoon grated orange rind
1 tablespoon flour
2 teaspoons chopped fresh parsley
Dash paprika
1 orange, peeled and sliced

Place chicken breasts, skin side up, on rack of broiler pan. Broil 2 inches from heat for 10 minutes or until skin is brown. Place browned chicken breasts in a shallow baking dish. Add salt and arrange mushrooms, onion and green peppers around chicken.

Combine orange juice, sherry, water, brown sugar, salt, pepper, orange rind and flour in small saucepan. Cook over medium heat, stirring constantly, until sauce thickens. Pour over chicken.

Bake in 375° oven 45 minutes or until chicken is done. Sprinkle with paprika and garnish with orange slices. Serves 6.

Spanada, Spices and Chicken

1 large fryer
½ pound fresh mushrooms
1 large onion
1 teaspoon salt
pepper
1 clove garlic minced
1 cup spanada (bottled wine & juice mixture)
1 cup chicken broth or bouillon
½ teaspoon rosemary

Cut up large fryer; roll chicken in flour. Brown in olive oil, add fresh mushrooms, onion. Saute together, drain fat; add salt, pepper, garlic, spanada, rosemary, and broth or bouillon. Simmer for 10 minutes. Serve in warm chafing dish. Garnish with pineapple and marachino cherries. Serves 4.

Chicken and Artichokes

1 large frying chicken, (cut up)
2 tablespoons olive oil
1 small onion, chopped
1 clove garlic, minced
1 teaspoon flour
1 cup hot chicken broth
1 tablespoon tomato paste
¼ cup chopped fresh parsley
1 teaspoon dried rosemary
1 teaspoon salt
¼ teaspoon pepper
6 fresh artichokes, cleaned and cut in half
1 cup white wine

In large skillet, brown chicken in oil. Transfer chicken to large baking pan. Brown onion and garlic in remaining oil. Slowly stir in flour; add broth, wine, tomato paste and seasonings. Add artichoke halves to sauce and simmer five minutes. Add wine and simmer 2 to 3 minutes. Arrange artichokes and chicken alternately in baking dish. Pour sauce over all. Bake at 325° until tender, about 45 minutes. Serves 4.

Lenten Scallops

⅓ cup sliced fresh mushrooms
1 tablespoon butter or margarine
1 tablespoon lemon juice
1 pound fresh or frozen scallops, rinsed well
2 tablespoons snipped chives
2 tablespoons chopped fresh parsley
½ cup dry white wine
¼ cup water
2 teaspoons cornstarch
¾ cup skim milk
Salt and pepper
1½ tablespoons fine dry bread crumbs
Paprika

In large skillet, cook mushrooms in butter and lemon juice 5 minutes. Add scallops, chives, parsley, wine and water. Cover and cook 5 minutes or until scallops are tender. Remove scallops and mushrooms with a slotted spoon, leaving liquid in pan. Mix the milk and cornstarch, add to the pan and cook until sauce thickens. Pour liquid and scallops into a shallow baking dish. Sprinkle with bread crumbs and paprika. Put under broiler or in preheated 375° oven for 5 minutes. Serves 4.

Marinated Lamb Roast

1 cup red wine
¼ cup olive oil
1 tablespoon wine vinegar
1 clove garlic, minced
½ teaspoon dried thyme
1 bay leaf
Salt and pepper
1 leg or shoulder of lamb

Combine all ingredients except lamb. Prick holes in lamb roast; place in roasting pan and pour marinade over. Let lamb marinate 4 to 5 hours in refrigerator (overnight if possible) before roasting, turning from time to time.

Roast according to meat thermometer at 325°, approximately 25 minutes per pound. Baste often with the marinade.

Garnish with mint leaves and cherry tomatoes.

Fresh Mint Sauce

Heat 2 tablespoons water and 1 tablespoon sugar until sugar is dissolved. Add ½ cup vinegar and 1/3 cup chopped fresh mint leaves.

Adds a festive, delicate touch to lamb and beef roasts. The simplest cut of chuck roast is transformed from ordinary to special with this pleasant sauce. Makes about 2/3 cup.

Stuffed Cornish Hens

½ cup butter or margarine
½ cup chopped celery
½ cup minced onions
1 pound fresh mushrooms, coarsely chopped
1 teaspoon salt or to taste
Pepper
2 cups cooked wild rice
4 Cornish hens, cleaned

Heat butter; add celery and onions and saute. Add mushrooms and saute briefly. Stir in salt and pepper and mix with cooked rice.

Sprinkle cavities of hens with salt. Spoon stuffing into birds. Secure with skewers or string. Arrange hens in shallow roasting pan and brush with butter. Roast at 325° about 1 hour.

Place on serving platter and garnish with orange slices or whole kumquats and green leaves. Serves 4.

Easter Crabmeat Pie

Filling

½ cup mayonnaise
2 eggs, beaten
½ cup milk
2 tablespoons flour
1 package (6 ounces) frozen crabmeat, thawed and drained
8 ounces Swiss cheese, cut into ¼-inch cubes
⅓ cup chopped green onions

Pie Shell

1 cup flour
½ teaspoon salt
⅓ cup plus 1 tablespoon shortening
2 to 3 tablespoons cold water

Make pastry: Combine ingredients; roll out pastry and put in greased 9-inch pan. If you wish, place a piece of buttered aluminum foil, buttered side down, over pastry shell; cover foil with dried peas. This will keep sides of shell from collapsing. Bake at 400° for 10 minutes. Remove the foil and peas; prick shell, then bake 3 to 5 minutes longer until lightly browned. Remove from oven. Reduce temperature to 350°.

Make filling: While pie shell cools combine mayonnaise, eggs, milk and flour; mix thoroughly. Stir in crabmeat, cheese and onions. Spoon into pie shell. Bake at 350° for 30 to 40 minutes, until center is firm. Serves 6.

Sicily, melting pot of many cultures, preserves her Temple of Concord.

Going back to Sicily at Easter reawakened a taste for the family's unique Easter celebration. Always included in our Spring celebration is a dish that is made exclusively in one small village in Sicily.

Tiano

Italian Easter Dish

The Italian Easter dish is called Tiano, and it is the specialty of the village of Aragona.

Abounding in eggs, it is made in a ring pan that is symbolic of eternal life. It is made only at Eastertime.

On Good Friday for centuries the families of the village have taken part in a procession originating in one of its small baroque churches and ending in the decorated village square. The patron saints of the village, Peter and Paul, are represented in huge paper-mache images. These are carried by local men at the head of the parade.

A saddened statue of the Blessed Lady is carried in the parade. Then on Easter Sunday a triumphant Christ is taken out of one of the seven small churches and together with a happy Virgin Mother is paraded to the village square.

In the homes Tiano is served. Unlike most southern Italian pasta dishes, the baked cake-like meal has no 'red' spaghetti sauce. It was originally baked in the communal city brick ovens, each family taking its turn at the oven. Its ingredients, like Sicily, represent the many cultures that have touched, ruled or plundered that island.

The cinnamon speaks of the Arab influence; the saffron is from the time of Spanish rule of the city by the Prince of Aragon. The pasta and meatballs are Italian, of course. And all together it is a dish that families look forward to each year.

Sicilian Tiano and chicken broth blend superbly.

I.

Prepare and fry this basic meatball mixture:

1 pound mixed ground beef and pork
1 cup Italian bread softened and squeezed dry
¾ cup grated Parmesan cheese
1 tablespoon minced fresh parsley
1 clove garlic
2 eggs
salt and pepper to taste

II.

½ pound Rigatoni macaroni

Boil until tender, but not overdone. Set aside. Grease round tube pan or casserole.

III.

Beat together:

1 dozen eggs
1 tablespoon parsley
1 cup Parmesan cheese
salt to taste
¼ teaspoon cinnamon

IV.

Prepare **chicken broth** with **½ teaspoon saffron.**

V.

2 pounds Munster cheese

Alternate pasta (each piece dipped in egg batter), followed by a layer of crumbled fried meat balls and a layer of Tuma (Munster cheese) sliced thinly and also dipped in egg batter. After each layer, 1 or 2 Tablespoons of chicken broth is poured over to bind and moisten it. The last layer is topped by the Tuma cheese and egg batter to glaze it. Bake at 325° for 1 to 1½ hours until golden brown. Serve hot or cold, cut in wedges. Delicious with tossed green salad.

The egg is as basic to life as any nutrient. It still remains one of our most economical sources of protein and happily it can be a celebrant's gourmet delight. Omelets can make a Sunday morning special or a plain Wednesday feel elegant.

Frittata

3 tablespoons olive oil
½ cup chopped onions
½ cup sliced mushrooms
½ cup sliced sweet peppers
Salt and pepper
6 eggs
¼ cup tomato sauce or grated Parmesan cheese

Heat oil in skillet. Saute onions, mushrooms and peppers 5 minutes. Beat eggs well and pour over vegetables; season. Slip spatula under omelet, letting liquid egg seep under. Cook until firm. Top with tomato sauce (or your favorite sauce) or Parmesan cheese.

The omelet may also be started in an ovenproof skillet on the range top, then baked at 350° until firm. Serves 4.

Variations

Cheeses make compatible marriages with eggs—one complementing the other in mellow ways. Parmesan, mozzarella, Cheddar and Swiss are also zestful companions for the golden, puffy protein. Ricotta also works well, melting delicately on a frittata.

Peppers and tomatoes, canned in early fall, were always perennial staples to transform a plain omelet into a hearty, delectable meal. Potatoes, cauliflower or zucchini are yet other possibilities.

The Italian Villages, roots of many traditional recipes.

Spinach and Ricotta Pie

Pastry for two-crust pie (or 2 frozen pastry
   shells, thawed)
2 pounds fresh spinach or 2 boxes (10 ounces each) frozen
   chopped spinach
2 tablespoons chopped onion
Olive oil
About 16 ounces ricotta cheese
1 cup milk
Salt
¼ cup butter or margarine
6 eggs
⅔ cup grated Parmesan cheese

Prepare favorite pastry recipe or use filo pastry. Line 9-inch
pie pan with bottom layer.

Cook spinach until just tender. Drain well and chop. Brown
onion in olive oil. Add spinach; saute just for a minute. Blend
milk and ricotta; season with salt.

Spread spinach mixture over bottom of crust. Add ricotta in
smooth layer. Make 6 holes with spoon for eggs. Dot each hole
with butter; carefully break egg into each. Sprinkle Parmesan
cheese over all. Put on top crust and flute edges. Bake at 375°
for 45 minutes until golden. Serve hot or cold. Serves 6.

*The pastoral beauty of
Italy produces slow
goats and good cheeses.*

As simple as the combination, the quick frying of one egg with bread smashed on it, provides a special taste of its own.

Fried Egg on Bread

1 tablespoon butter
1 egg
1 slice favorite bread
Garnish—cheese
Canadian bacon and/or tomatoes (optional)

Melt the butter in flat skillet or on grill. Drop egg on butter. Place slice of bread on top. Flatten gently with spatula. Flip and toast other side gently. Serve hot.

Cheese or Canadian bacon on top adds another dimension. For a festive flair on a holiday weekend, broil ½ tomato with 1 tablespoon butter and serve on your favorite luncheon plate with the F.E.O.B.—about 300 calories! Serves 1.

Spinach and Cheese Gnocchi

½ pound fresh spinach leaves or 1 box (10 ounces) frozen chopped spinach
1 tablespoon butter or margarine, melted
1 cup ricotta cheese
½ cup grated Parmesan cheese
3 egg yolks, lightly beaten
1 teaspoon salt
Pepper
Flour seasoned with nutmeg
Additional butter and grated Parmesan cheese

Cook spinach in 1 tablespoon butter until tender; chop spinach (if using fresh). Mix well with cheeses, egg yolks, salt and pepper. Chill for about 1 hour. Form walnut size balls; roll in flour. Drop a few at a time into large pan of boiling water; when they rise to the top, they are done. Remove with slotted spoon to a buttered shallow baking dish. Dot with butter and sprinkle with cheese. Bake at 350° for 20 minutes. Serves 4.

Ricotta Gnocchi

A good side dish with lamb or pork.

About 16 ounces ricotta cheese
½ cup grated Parmesan cheese
¼ cup butter or margarine, softened
4 eggs, well beaten
⅓ cup flour
½ teaspoon salt
Dash pepper
Chicken broth or salted water

Mix all ingredients except broth or water until blended. Form balls about size of golf balls. Drop into boiling broth or salted water. Let cook until the gnocchi float on top (about 7 minutes). Remove with slotted spoon. Toss gently with butter and grated Parmesan cheese. Serves 8.

Spaghetti with Fresh Vegetables

Pastas

Basic tomato sauce (page 24)
1½ pounds spaghetti

Choice of vegetable:
1 small head cauliflower, broken into flowerettes
2 cups cut-up fresh asparagus
2 cups cut-up fresh green beans
2 cups shelled fresh peas
2 stalks fresh broccoli, cut up

Prepare tomato sauce. Cook spaghetti in boiling salted water. Meanwhile, steam vegetable of your choice until just tender. Drain spaghetti. Dress with tomato sauce, then top with vegetable. Sprinkle with grated Parmesan cheese, if you wish. Serves 4 to 6.

This dish can become an art focus in itself; flower petals for the eye, pasta for the palate.

Eggplant with Spaghetti

6 medium eggplants
Salt
3 tablespoons olive oil
2 cloves garlic
2 pounds ripe tomatoes or 2 cans (16 ounces each) plum tomatoes chopped (reserve liquid)
2 or 3 sprigs fresh basil, chopped, or 1 teaspoon dried basil
2 pounds spaghetti
Pepper
¾ cup grated Parmesan cheese

Peel eggplant and cut in thin slices. Sprinkle with salt and let set 1 hour. Wipe dry. Heat oil in large skillet and saute eggplant. Remove and drain on paper towels. Saute garlic in the oil; discard garlic. Add tomatoes, their liquid and seasonings; heat.

Meanwhile, cook spaghetti in boiling salted water. Drain; pour tomato sauce over. Arrange petals of fried eggplant on top and sprinkle with Parmesan cheese. Serves 6-8.

Fettuccini with Zucchini and Mushrooms

½ pound fresh mushrooms, sliced
¼ cup butter or margarine
1½ pounds zucchini, sliced
1 egg, lightly beaten
1 cup light cream or half-and-half
1 teaspoon chopped fresh parsley
½ teaspoon salt
¼ teaspoon nutmeg
1 pound fettuccini
1 cup grated Parmesan cheese

In large skillet, saute mushrooms in butter until soft, about 2 or 3 minutes. Add zucchini. Stirring occasionally, let vegetables cook gently, for about five minutes or until just tender. Beat egg into cream and add to vegetables along with parsley, salt and nutmeg.

Cook fettuccini in boiling salted water. Drain well. Place in warm serving dish or deep round casserole. Add hot vegetables in cream sauce, tossing gently. Sprinkle with Parmesan cheese, toss and serve immediately. Serves 4.

Spaghettini with Cheese Sauce

1 onion, chopped
2 tablespoons butter or margarine
½ cup milk
1 cup ricotta cheese
4 ounces gorgonzola cheese, chopped
1 pound spaghettini
1 teaspoon paprika

Brown onion in butter. Add milk gradually to ricotta cheese.
Add gorgonzola to ricotta mixture. Slowly pour cheese mix-
ture into browned onions and heat gently. Cook spaghettini in
boiling salted water. Drain and toss with the cheese sauce.
Sprinkle with paprika. Serve with grated Parmesan cheese.
Serves 4.

Stuffed Eggplant Cartwheels

1 pound eggplant, peeled
2 eggs, well beaten
½ cup milk
½ cup flour
½ teaspoon salt
Olive oil
1 cup ricotta or farmer's cheese
2 tablespoons chopped fresh parsley
1½ cups Basic Tomato Sauce (page 24)
¼ cup grated Parmesan cheese
Salt and pepper

Cut eggplant into ⅛-inch-thick slices. Sprinkle with salt and
let stand for an hour. Pat slices dry with paper towels. Combine eggs and milk. Blend flour and salt. Dip eggplant slices
into egg mixture, then into flour. Heat a little oil in a large
skillet and saute eggplant slices, a few at a time, until golden
brown. Drain on paper towels. Spread each slice with about 1
tablespoon ricotta cheese; roll up like a jelly roll and secure
with a toothpick. Place rolls in a buttered 13x9-inch baking
dish. Top with tomato sauce and sprinkle with Parmesan
cheese. Bake at 350° for 20 minutes. Serves 4.

These little gems can finish a meat platter as elegantly as a perfect strand of pearls finishes a simple dress.

Rosemary Potatoes

3 tablespoons butter or margarine, melted
2 tablespoons olive or salad oil
10 small new potatoes, peeled
1 teaspoon dried rosemary, crushed
1 teaspoon salt
⅛ teaspoon black pepper (optional)

Combine butter and oil. Place the potatoes in a casserole and pour butter mixture over. Sprinkle with seasonings. Bake in a 400° oven, uncovered, for 45 minutes, or until crispy and brown. Serves 3 or 4.

Puffed Mushrooms

1 pound medium mushrooms
2 eggs, beaten
1½ cups plain pancake mix (dry)
Oil for deep-frying
Salt

Wash and trim mushrooms, leaving on the stems. Roll the mushrooms in the beaten eggs, then in the pancake mix. Heat oil and deep-fry mushrooms about 4 to 5 minutes. Remove with slotted spoon to paper towels; drain. Sprinkle with salt to taste. Serves 4.

Parmesan Cauliflower

1 head cauliflower, separated into flowerettes
2 eggs, well beaten
½ cup seasoned fine bread crumbs
Olive oil
½ cup Parmesan cheese

Steam cauliflower or cook in boiling salted water until just tender. Dip each flowerette in beaten eggs, then in bread crumbs. Heat oil in large skillet. Add cauliflower and saute, turning, until golden. Remove with slotted spoon and sprinkle with cheese. Serves 4.

Easter Cassata

(Italian Cream Cake)

Desserts

Cassata

1¼ cup sugar
1 cup butter
6 egg yolks
2 cups sifted cake flour
½ teaspoon baking powder
½ teaspoon salt
½ cup milk
6 egg whites
¾ cup sugar

Cream butter and 1 cup sugar until light and fluffy, about 7 minutes. Add egg yolks one at a time and beat well after each addition, about 5 minutes. Add dry ingredients alternating with ½ cup milk, beating well after each addition. Beat egg whites until soft peaks form. Fold into batter. Pour into 10" tube pan and bake at 350° for 50 to 55 minutes. Invert on bottle and cool. Cut cake in three layers.

Cassata filling

¾ cups sugar
3 tablespoons cornstarch
¾ cup milk
16 ounces ricotta cheese
2 tablespoons orange liqueur
1½ teaspoon vanilla
½ cup chopped semi-sweet chocolate
¼ cup finely chopped candies citron

Combine ¾ cup sugar, butter and cornstarch in saucepan. Stir in ¾ cup milk and cook stirring constantly until thickened and bubbly. Remove from heat and cover with wax paper and cool. In electric mixer, beat ricotta cheese until creamy. Blend into cooked cornstarch mixture, add orange liqueur and vanilla. Stir in chopped chocolate and citron. Spread between layers of cake.

Chocolate frosting for Cassata

Melt 2-3 ounces unsweetened chocolate and 2-3 tablespoon butter. Add ½ cup hot coffee, ⅛ teaspoon salt. Add about 2 cups confectioners sugar and 1 teaspoon vanilla. Beat until smooth. Frost top and sides of Cassata. Sprinkle nuts around sides of cake. Chill. Makes 16 servings.

Cannoli

Cannoli Shells

1¾ cups unsifted flour
½ teaspoon salt
2 tablespoons granulated sugar
1 egg, lightly beaten
2 tablespoons firm butter or margarine, cut in small pieces
¼ cup dry Sauterne
1 egg white, lightly beaten
Shortening or salad oil for deep-frying
Filling (below)
Powdered sugar
Chopped sweet chocolate and halved candied cherries for garnish

Sift flour with salt and granulated sugar. Make a well in the center of flour mixture; in it place egg and butter. Stir with a fork, working from center out, to moisten dry ingredients. Add wine, 1 tablespoon at a time, until dough begins to cling together. Use your hands to form dough into a ball. Cover and let stand for 15 minutes.

Roll dough out about 1/16 inch thick on floured board. Cut into 3½-inch circles. Roll circles into ovals. Wrap around cannoli forms; seal edge with egg white. Turn out ends of dough to flare slightly. Fry two or three at a time in deep hot fat (350°) for about 1 minute or until lightly golden. Remove with tongs to paper towels to drain. Let cool about 5 seconds; then slip out cannoli form, holding shell carefully. Cool shells compelely before filling. Use pastry tube to fill. Sift powdered sugar over shells; garnish at ends. Makes 25.

Ricotta Filling

Whirl 32 ounces (4 cups) ricotta cheese in the blender or press through wire strainer until very smooth. Beat in 1½ cups unsifted powdered sugar and 4 teaspoons vanilla. Mix in ½ cup each finely chopped citron and orange peel and ¼ cup chopped sweet chocolate. Chill several hours or overnight.

Fluffy Ricotta Filling

Prepare ½ recipe Ricotta Filling (above), then fold in 1 cup heavy cream, beaten until stiff.

Pistachio Filling

To either of the above filling recipes add a few drops green food coloring to tint pale green. Use chopped blanched pistachio nuts for garnish.

Easter Lamb Cake

2¼ cups sifted cake flour
1½ cups sugar
3½ teaspoons baking powder
1 teaspoon salt
½ cup shortening
1 cup milk
1 teaspoon vanilla
2 eggs

Have all ingredients at room temperature. Sift dry ingredients into large mixing bowl. Add shortening, ⅔ cup of the milk and the vanilla. Beat for about 2 minutes. Add remaining ⅓ milk and unbeaten eggs. Beat 2 minutes. Pour into 13x9-inch baking dish or two small lamb-shaped cake pans. Bake in 350° oven for 30 to 35 minutes. Let cool.

Top oblong cake with Pineapple Topping (below). Or: Fasten lamb halves together with frosting or filling, then frost with white frosting and sprinkle with shredded coconut. Use black jelly beans for eyes (and tie a pretty ribbon gently around the neck).

Pineapple Topping

1 can (20 ounces) crushed pineapple
3 tablespoons cornstarch
¼ cup water
½ cup sugar
⅛ teaspoon salt
1 egg yolk, beaten

Drain pineapple, reserving syrup. Blend cornstarch with water until smooth. Blend sugar and salt into pineapple syrup and bring to a boil. Add cornstarch mixture, stirring constantly until thickened. Mix 2 tablespoons of the thickened sauce with egg yolk and return to the pan. Do not boil, but blend well. Let cool and add crushed pineapple. Spread over cool cake.

Grapes Supreme

Just enough after a heavy meal!

½ cup seedless green grapes
2 teaspoons brown sugar
2 teaspoons sour cream

Rinse grapes, then place in berry dish or antique bowl. Sprinkle brown sugar evenly over grapes and top with sour cream. Serve with plain cookies. Makes 1 serving.

A delicacy that can be varied with your favorite filling.

Mary's Meringue Pastry

3 cups flour
3 tablespoons sugar
1 cup butter or margarine, softened
1 packet dry yeast
1 cup warm milk
4 eggs separated
1½ cups sugar
Fillings: small nuts, raisins, cherries, shredded coconut and/or chocolate chips

Combine flour and 3 tablespoons sugar. Work butter into mixture with pastry cutter. Dissolve yeast in warm milk. Add yolks and yeast-milk mixture. Place in refrigerator for at least 2 hours. Divide dough into 3 balls. Roll each section out to ⅛ inch thickness.

Beat egg whites until stiff, adding 1½ cups sugar slowly. Spread ⅓ of this meringue over each pastry. Add ⅓ of your favorite filling to each. Roll up into jelly rolls. Place on floured cookie sheet. Let set in warm place 1 hour to rise. Bake at 350° for 20 minutes. Sift powdered sugar on top or make icing: Mix 1 cup powdered sugar, 2 tablespoons butter or margarine, and warm water to spreadable consistency. Serves 24.

Ricotta Pie

Pie Crust

1½ cups flour
¾ cup shortening
3 teaspoons baking powder
3 tablespoons water
1 teaspoon salt

Filling

16 ounces ricotta cheese
2 eggs
½ cup sugar
¼ teaspoon salt
1 teaspoon vanilla, lemon juice or nutmeg
Citron (optional)

Mix together pie crust ingredients. Roll out two crusts. Line pie pan with one. Combine ricotta, eggs, sugar and salt. Vary flavoring according to favorite taste. (Citron may also be added.) Top with second crust. Bake at 450° for 20 minutes until lightly brown, then reduce to 350° and continue baking for 20 minutes. Serves 8.

Peaches and Marsala

There are many versions of peach desserts, but one of the simplest yet most elegant came to us from a friend from Florence. There, she boasts, things are done in the purest Italian form. A carefully chosen, choice peach, peeled and placed in a sherbet glass, is the first step. Simply pour 3 tablespoons Marsala wine over each. Top with real whipped cream. An easy but superb ending to any meal!

Calabrian Easter Bread

1½ cakes yeast dissolved in 2 cups warm water
5 pounds flour (all purpose)
1½ cups sugar
8 eggs
2 tablespoons salt
2 sticks margarine
1 pint milk

Hard boiled eggs are often placed on this golden braid for an added Easter symbol.

Heat together milk, margarine, sugar and salt. Set aside.

Beat eggs well, add a few drops of yellow food coloring for a richer color. Fold in half of flour to egg mixture. Then add water and yeast as well as warm milk mixture. Fold in remaining flour; let rise 1 hour or until doubled in size.

Shape into twisted rings or rolls; let rise 1 hour again.

Brush with 1 whole egg and 1 tablespoon milk—well blended. Bake at 350° for 20-30 minutes.

Calabrian Easter Bread adds elegance to Sunday morning.

Anise Toast

2½ cups flour
2 teaspoons baking powder
¼ teaspoon salt
¼ cup butter or margarine, softened
1 cup sugar
3 eggs
1 tablespoon anise extract

Sift flour with baking powder and salt three times; set aside. In medium bowl, beat butter and sugar until light and fluffy. Add eggs, one at a time, beating well after each addition. Add anise and flour mixture. Divide dough in half and spread half on greased cookie sheet. Bake 15 to 20 minutes at 350°. Remove from oven and slice into 1-inch-thick slices. Turn each piece over and bake 10 to 15 minutes longer. Slices should be slightly brown. Makes about 24 slices.

An easy dessert for those unexpected guests.

Ricotta-Stuffed Peaches

6 fresh peaches, peeled and cut in half
Granulated sugar to frost peaches
8 ounces ricotta cheese
1 teaspoon vanilla or almond liqueur
¼ cup sugar
12 maraschino cherries

Gently dip peach halves into bowl of warm water, then in bowl of sugar for a frosted coating. Combine ricotta, flavoring and ¼ cup sugar. Pipe or spoon ricotta mixture onto each peach half. Top with cherries. Serves 6.

Homemade Ricotta

1 gallon milk
1 cup water
½ cup white vinegar

Scald the milk and remove from heat. In another pan, heat the water and vinegar until hot (do not boil). Pour water/vinegar mixture over milk, a little at a time. The milk will separate and form curds. Scoop out the curds with a slotted spoon or strainer.

Summer

Summertime, with its humid afternoons and lazy sunsets, is that special season for cold fruits, ices, and fresh foods, simply prepared. It is a time for foods quickly procured, plucked from nearby gardens, eaten in natural forms or roasted gently out of doors. It is a time for foods shared in the open air, as groups gather on the patios and in the parks for summer reunions. It is a time for foods eaten for no other reason than the freshness of their taste—a tomato juicy from the vine, berries picked in the field, a tart apple from the tree.

People gathering on these melting days enjoy a spontaneity that can be mirrored by the simplicity and freshness of the foods—the barbecue, with everyone cooking together in the open air; the ice cream social; the neighborhood picnic.

Tasty foods that can be quickly prepared are available. Summer dishes capitalize on the peak of ripeness of every growing thing: Leafy lettuce from the gardens. Corn, sweet in itself. Potatoes and green beans, at their best in cold salads. Chickens marinated in fresh lemon juice and oregano, then cooked over coals with the roasted ears of corn.

My childhood memories of summer are easily re-created for our summer guests with roasted chickens, pitchers of frosted lemonade, watermelon in ice buckets, and finally the churning of ice cream by many small hands. My own father would never give in to the electric machine, and my sons excitedly perpetuate the tradition. Half the calories can be eliminated from ice cream, and twice the conviviality can be added—and always the taste is improved by the churning of the rich cream.

The colors of summer foods are brilliant! Picture skewers of marinated chunks of beef or lamb, yellow pineapples, rich red tomatoes, dark green peppers, and plump mushrooms. Turning on the orange embers, they are a colorful sight, artistic as well as appetizing.

Torches glowing on the patio give a mellowness to the warm evenings of the season. And just before the last embers flicker, there is a perfect temperature for roasting puffy marshmallows, a sweet and gentle ending to the summer and its good foods.

Caesar Salad Gaziano

1 bunch Romaine lettuce
½ head iceberg lettuce
3 tablespoons olive oil
⅛ teaspoon minced garlic
Salt
½ teaspoon coarse black pepper
1 egg, well beaten
1 tablespoon vinegar or lemon juice
1 cup croutons or cut-up bread sticks
¼ cup grated Parmesan cheese
1 can (2 ounces) anchovy fillets, drained
8 to 10 green olives

Rinse and drain lettuce leaves and tear into bite-size pieces. Combine both kinds in large wooden bowl. Mix oil, garlic, salt and pepper and sprinkle over lettuce, tossing lightly. Add well-beaten egg and toss; add vinegar and toss well. Sprinkle with croutons and Parmesan cheese. Garnish with anchovy fillets and olives. Serves 6 to 8. Optional: croutons may be soaked in olive oil and garlic.

Salads

Large, clear bowls show off this salad's beauty; a wonderfully satisfying light meal by itself.

Cool Orange-Shrimp Salad

Lettuce leaves
1 pound small shrimp, cooked and cleaned
1 cup chopped celery
2 small green onions, chopped
¼ cup mayonnaise
2 oranges, peeled and cut in half, then sliced
1 tablespoon lemon juice
1 tablespoon sugar
2 tablespoons chopped fresh parsley
1 cucumber, peeled and sliced thin

Line a shallow bowl with lettuce leaves. Combine shrimp, celery, onions and mayonnaise. Add oranges and pour mixture onto lettuce leaves. Mix lemon juice, sugar and parsley. Toss with cucumbers. Arrange cucumbers on top of shrimp mixture. Serves 4.

Tart and tangy tuna adds fun to plain protein.

Lemony Tuna Salad

2 cans (6 to 8 ounes each) tuna, drained and flaked
2 medium tomatoes, cut into wedges
1 small onion, sliced
Juice of 1 lemon
1 lemon, cut into very thin wedges
Leaf lettuce

Combine tuna, tomatoes and onion. Sprinkle with lemon juice. Toss lemon wedges into salad. Serve on bed of leaf lettuce. Serves 4.

Tomato and Crushed Red Pepper Salad

Rub a small bowl with a garlic clove. Choose 5 or 6 plump, sweet, ripe tomatoes. Cut into wedges and place in bowl. Blend ½ cup olive oil, ½ teaspoon crushed red pepper and ½ teaspoon dried oregano. Pour over tomatoes and toss gently. Serves 4.

Vegetables, dairy product and protein in pleasant company.

Mushroom, Provolone and Ham Salad

1 pound fresh mushrooms
½ pound ham, prosciutto or salami
½ pound provolone cheese
1 clove garlic
½ cup olive oil
¼ cup vinegar

Clean mushrooms and slice. Cut ham and cheese in 2x¼-inch strips. Rub garlic clove in serving bowl, then crush in the oil. Blend oil and vinegar and pour over mushrooms. Top with strips of ham and cheese. Serves 4.

Honey-Lime Fruit Salad

Fruit superbly dressed is summer!

Prepare about 4 cups seasonal fresh fruits: pineapple, melon, peaches, banana, apples, oranges, grapefruit. Peel and cut into sections or chunks; chill.

Using a chilled bowl and beaters, beat ½ cup chilled whipping cream or Dream Whip until it stands in stiff peaks. Blend 3 tablespoons honey and 2 or 3 teaspoons lime, lemon or orange juice; beat into whipped cream with as few strokes as possible. Serve over chilled fruit in compote or antique glass bowl. Serves 6.

Artichoke and Avocado Salad

Green and golden, this cooling salad is another summer winner!

Combine 1 cup canned or thawed frozen artichoke hearts, 1 large avocado, peeled and cut into wedges, and 1 grapefruit, peeled and sectioned. Toss with Italian dressing. Serve in lettuce cups or in lettuce-lined salad bowl. Serves 4.

Cauliflower Salad

When the garden overflows with green gems, try this.

1 medium head cauliflower
¼ cup olive or salad oil
3 tablespoons red wine vinegar
1 tablespoon chopped green onions
1 tablespoon diced pimiento (optional)
1 teaspoon dried thyme
½ teaspoon salt
¼ teaspoon pepper

Break the cauliflower into flowerettes and steam or cook in boiling water until just tender. Do not overcook. Drain and chill in refrigerator. Mix remaining ingredients and pour over cauliflower, tossing lightly to blend the flavors. Serve in individual dishes or salad bowl. Serves 4 to 6.

Spinach and Mandarin Orange Salad

1 pound fresh spinach
1 can (6 ounces) mandarin oranges, drained
3 tablespoons oil
2 tablespoons cider vinegar
1 teaspoon lemon juice
2 tablespoons sugar
¼ cup slivered almonds

Rinse spinach leaves and tear into bite-size pieces. Add oranges. Blend oil, vinegar, lemon juice and sugar; pour over salad. Garnish with slivered almonds. Serves 4.

Cucumbers in Sour Cream

1 large cucumber, peeled and sliced
¾ teaspoon salt
½ cup dairy sour cream
Vinegar to taste
1 tablespoon sugar
¼ teaspoon dried dillweed
Dash pepper

Sprinkle cucumber with salt. Combine remaining ingredients and pour over salted cucumbers. Serves 2 to 4.

Spinach and Mushroom Salad

1 pound fresh spinach
½ pound fresh mushrooms
2 tomatoes
¼ cup olive oil
3 tablespoons vinegar
Salt and pepper
Bacon-flavored chips

Rinse spinach leaves. Slice mushrooms and cut tomatoes into wedges. Blend oil, vinegar, salt and pepper. Toss with vegetables. Sprinkle with bacon-flavored chips. Serves 4.

Zucchini Salad

2 pounds zucchini
3 tablespoons olive oil
2 tablespoons vinegar
½ green pepper, cut into thin strips
1 teaspoon chopped fresh parsley
Salt and pepper

Steam or boil zucchini until just tender/not mushy. Pat dry. Cube or slice into bite-size pieces. Blend oil and vinegar, pour over zucchini and toss. Add strips of pepper and sprinkle with parsley. Serves 4 to 6.

Summer Special Salad Dressing

4 eggs
3 cups sugar
2 cups cider vinegar
1 tablespoon dry or Dijon mustard
⅛ teaspoon turmeric

Beat eggs with sugar. Stir in vinegar. Cook in saucepan, over medium heat, stirring just until thickened. Do not boil. Cool, then stir in seasonings. Store in refrigerator. Makes about 4 cups.

This favorite dressing of my aunt transforms simple potato salad from ordinary picnic fare into the life of the party.

Tabooleh for Italian Feasts

1 cup bulgur (cracked) wheat
5 tomatoes
1 bunch green onions
2 large bunches parsley
1 cup fresh mint leaves
Juice of 3 lemons
¼ cup olive oil
Salt and pepper

Rinse the wheat and soak in plenty of water for 10 minutes. Clean and chop all vegetables. With your hands, squeeze water from wheat and add to vegetables. Add lemon juice, oil, salt and pepper and mix well. Serves 4 to 6.

Barbeques

Strips of green pepper and a little garlic produce a tasty variation of the economical American bird.

Pollo Fritto
(Italian Fried Chicken)

1 fryer (3 to 4 pounds), cut into serving pieces
½ cup flour
1 teaspoon salt
Dash pepper
About 1 cup combination oils (¾ cup vegetable oil, ¼ cup olive oil)
1 clove garlic
Dash paprika
2 green peppers, cut up

Dredge chicken pieces in flour (or pour flour in paper bag; add chicken pieces, a few at a time, and shake well). Sprinkle chicken with salt and pepper. Heat about ¼ inch oil in heavy skillet. Saute garlic and remove. Add chicken and brown on one side; turn and sprinkle with paprika. Add green peppers. Slowly fry chicken and pepper pieces until crisp and done. (About ½ hour) Serves 4 to 6.

Scampi alla Griglia
(Skewered Shrimp)

2 pounds scampi or shrimp, boiled and shelled
¾ cup olive oil
2 cloves garlic, minced
2 tablespoons minced parsley
¾ teaspoon salt
½ teaspoon freshly ground black pepper
1 green pepper, cut into 1-inch squares
½ pound cherry tomatoes

Rinse shrimp; shell and devein. Mix oil, garlic, parsley, salt and pepper. Marinate the scampi in mixture for 1 hour in refrigerator, turning frequently.

Alternate shrimp on skewers with green pepper pieces and cherry tomatoes. Cook over charcoal, basting with remaining marinade, until done, about 10 minutes. (Or broil in oven, if desired.) Serves 4 to 6.

Summer Steak Shish Kebabs

A ribbon of color: lovely to look at and scrumptious to the palate.

Marinade

1 cup red wine (Chianti, Burgundy)
1 cup vegetable oil
1 can (6 ounce) tomato sauce
2 tablespoons vinegar
2 teaspoons Worcestershire sauce
2 tablespoons sugar
1 clove garlic, minced
1 teaspoon salt
½ teaspoon rosemary

Shish Kebabs

2 pounds sirloin steak, cut into 2-inch cubes
1 pound mushrooms
1 pound cherry tomatoes
3 large onions, cut into 1-inch cubes
1 can (16 ounces) pineapple chunks, drained
2 green peppers, cut into 1-inch squares

Combine marinade ingredients in saucepan and simmer 20 minutes until slightly thickened. Cool. Pour over steak cubes, mixing well, and marinate at least two hours in refrigerator, turning occasionally.

Alternate beef on skewers with remaining shish kebab ingredients. Cook over charcoal, basting frequently with remaining marinade. Serves 4 to 6.

Shish kebabs: roasted on embers, a tasty and colorful must for summer.

Seafood Kabobs

1 pound cod fillets, cut into 1-inch cubes
1 pound medium shrimp, cleaned and deveined and boiled
1 pound scallops, rinsed
2 green peppers, cut into 1-inch squares
16 cherry tomatoes
4 small onions, cut in half
½ cup olive oil
¼ cup wine vinegar
1 teaspoon minced parsley

Alternate seafood and vegetables on skewers. Blend oil, vinegar and parsley and brush kabobs well with mixture. Broil over charcoal, basting with any remaining sauce. Serves 6 to 8.

Grilled Chicken Oregano

1 plump fryer, cut into serving pieces
½ cup butter or margarine
Juice of 2 lemons
3 tablespoons oregano

Place chicken parts in shallow baking dish. In small saucepan, melt butter and blend in lemon juice and oregano. Pour over chicken. Cook over hot coals, turning and basting often, or broil in oven. Serves 4 to 6.

Summer Zucchini in Batter

1 pound zucchini
2 eggs
½ cup flour
dash salt
cinnamon

When the zucchini is large and succulent, clean, peel and slice ½ inch thick.

Prepare egg batter (well beaten eggs, adding dash salt and cinnamon) Dip in flour, fry in hot fat, drain and serve hot and crisp. Serves 4.

Asparagus with Parmesan Cheese

Rob the garden at the peak of tenderness for an unforgettable vegetable.

2 pounds fresh or frozen asparagus tips
½ cup melted butter or margarine
½ cup grated Parmesan cheese

Cut off tough ends of asparagus. Steam or simmer until a little less than done. Drain well. Arrange in single layer in shallow baking dish. Pour melted butter over. Sprinkle with cheese. Bake at 400° for 10 minutes or until lightly browned. Serves 6.

New Potatoes and Green Beans

Summer soul food for Italian and garden lovers.

6 to 8 new potatoes
1 pound fresh green beans, cooked and drained
(or use canned)
1 small onion, chopped
3 tablespoons olive oil

Boil potatoes in their jackets. Meanwhile, brown onion in oil. When potatoes are tender, peel under cool water and cut up. Combine with green beans. Pour onion-oil mixture over potatoes and beans. Serve hot.

For variety, add 1 tablespoon vinegar to cooked onions. Chill and serve as a salad. Serves 4 to 6.

Midsummer Vegetable Marinade

½ head cauliflower
1 pound broccoli, cut into pieces
½ pound mushrooms
½ pound fresh or canned green beans
4 small carrots, cut into lengthwise quarters
1 cup cider vinegar
½ cup oil
⅓ cup sugar

Parboil fresh vegetables for 4 minutes. Drain and let cool. Blend vinegar, oil and sugar; pour over vegetables. Place in refrigerator for 24 hours. Keeps two weeks. Serves 8-10.

A New England secret to be shared with your family when corn is at its midsummer freshest!

Charcoal-Roasted Corn on the Cob

Remove all but one layer of corn husk from 1 dozen ears of fresh corn. Soak corn in pan of water until thoroughly moistened. Lay corn on charcoal grill. Cover with wet towels or feed sacks. Let steam and roast 45 minutes, turning 2 or 3 times.

Zucchini or Eggplant
in Tomato Sauce

1 clove garlic
3 tablespoons olive oil
1 can (16 ounces) Italian plum tomatoes
½ teaspoon salt
½ teaspoon pepper
2 pounds zucchini or eggplant, peeled and cut into cubes
½ cup grated Parmesan cheese
2 tablespoons chopped fresh basil or ½ teaspoon dried basil

Brown garlic in olive oil. Add undrained tomatoes; simmer until reduced to a thick sauce, stirring constantly. Season with salt and pepper. Add zucchini or eggplant and simmer, covered, until tender. Sprinkle with grated cheese and basil. Serves 4 to 6.

Traditional Homemade Ice Cream

2 cups milk
3 egg yolks
1 cup sugar
¼ teaspoon salt
2 cups heavy cream
4 teaspoons vanilla

Ices & Cool Desserts

The process is fun and the product delicious for the young and young at heart.

Scald milk. In a bowl, beat egg yolks, sugar and salt. Pour hot milk over egg mixture, stirring constantly. Return to the pan. Cook until mixture coats spoon. Add cream and vanilla. Churn in ice cream maker until firm and thick. Makes 2 quarts.

The churning of little hands make tasty gellata.

Top with your favorite summer fruit—a beauty!

Our Favorite Cheesecake
Crumb Crust

21 graham crackers, crushed (1½ cups)
1 tablespoon sugar
1 tablespoon butter or margarine, softened

Filling

3 packages (8 ounces each) cream cheese, softened
1 cup sugar
5 eggs
1½ teaspoons vanilla

Topping

1 pint sour cream
¼ cup sugar
1 teaspoon vanilla

Blend crust ingredients and press into pie plate.

Make filling: With electric mixer, beat cream cheese until light and fluffy, adding sugar gradually while beating. Beat in eggs, one at a time. Pour into crust and bake in a preheated 350° oven **exactly** 50 minutes.

Just before removing cheesecake from oven, blend topping ingredients. Spread over cheesecake and return to oven for 5 minutes only. Let cool, then chill in refrigerator or freezer. Serves 8.

Biscuit Tortoni

1 cup heavy cream
¼ cup powdered sugar
1 egg white, stiffly beaten
½ cup crumbled macaroons
2 teaspoons sherry

Beat cream until stiff. Fold in powdered sugar, then egg white, alternating with crumbled macaroons and sherry. Pack the mixture in 6 individual paper muffin cups. Sprinkle the tops with additional macaroon crumbs and set in refrigerator tray; freeze. Do not stir. Serves 6.

Chocolate Cups for Ice Cream

Heat 6 ounces semisweet chocolate and 2 tablespoons butter in top of double boiler over hot water until just melted. Mix well with a dry spoon. Place 6 paper muffin cups in tins. Using back of spoon, coat paper cups with chocolate, covering thinly and thoroughly. Cool in refrigerator or freezer. Peel off paper when ready to serve. Add a scoop of ice or sherbet. Top with a cherry. Makes 6.

A doily on the saucer makes this delightful for the dinner; no baking makes it delightful for the cook.

Chocolate Ladyfinger Torte

24 ladyfingers
1 cup almond liqueur or rum
½ teaspoon vanilla
8 ounces semisweet chocolate
3 to 4 tablespoons light cream
1 cup sweet butter, softened
⅓ cup sugar
2 egg yolks, lightly beaten
Blanched almond halves
Candied cherries
Whipped cream

Slit ladyfingers and place on platter. Sprinkle with the liqueur or rum and let soak for at least 2 hours (should retain shape). Combine chocolate, cream and vanilla in top of double boiler. Melt over hot water. Cream butter and sugar until fluffy and thoroughly blended. Gradually add egg yolks, mixing well. Add chocolate mixture to butter mixture, a little at a time; blend thoroughly until mixture is soft and creamy. Do not undermix.

To make torte, arrange a layer of 8 ladyfingers in form of square on a flat platter or cake plate. Spread with thin layer of chocolate cream. Repeat process, 2 more times finishing with layer of chocolate. Coat sides with chocolate. Decorate with almonds and cherries. Let ripen 12 hours in refrigerator. Let stand at room temperature 30 minutes before serving. Decorate with whipped cream just before serving. Serves 6 to 8.

Spumoni

3 cups heavy cream
¾ cup sugar, sifted
1¼ cups blanched almonds, sliced and toasted
4 ounces (4 squares) semisweet chocolate, chopped
1 tablespoon brandy or rum (optional)

Grease and line 9x5x3-inch loaf pan, or round mold, or use 16 paper-lined muffin cups. Beat cream until stiff. Gradually beat in sugar. (Do not overbeat.) Gently fold in almonds, chocolate and brandy. Pour mixture in prepared pan. Freeze, unmold and cut in thin slices. Serves 6.

Wonderful when you're rushed and the guests are due any minute.

Instant Spumoni

Soften 1 pint vanilla ice cream. Stir in 1 tablespoon rum and ¼ cup chopped candied fruits. Spoon into 8 paper-lined muffin cups. Return to freezer to firm. Serves 8.

Frank's Fruit Ice Cream

1 cup sugar
1 tablespoon cornstarch
¼ teaspoon salt
2 cups milk, scalded
3 eggs, beaten
1 cup whipping cream
2 teaspoons vanilla
2 cups cut-up fresh fruit

Blend sugar, cornstarch and salt. Add the hot milk and cook over hot water 10 minutes, stirring often. Add gradually to the beaten eggs, stirring constantly, then return to the double boiler and cook 3 minutes longer. Cool. Whip the cream until stiff; fold into custard along with vanilla. Add peaches, strawberries, or fruit of your choice. Freeze. Makes 1½ quarts.

Lemon Ice

1½ cups sugar
2½ cups water
1½ cups lemon juice
Pinch salt

Combine sugar and water. Bring to a boil, stir in lemon juice, making sure juice is thoroughly blended. Follow procedure as indicated in Strawberry Ice.

Strawberry Ice

2½ cups sugar
4 cups water
1 qt. ripe strawberries

Combine sugar and water. Bring to boil. Let dissolved mixture boil 15 minutes. Mash or puree strawberries for smooth ice (leave chunks if desired). Add sugar syrup to strawberries. Pour mixture in hand freezer or in deep tray in freezer. If the freezer ice tray is used - take tray out periodically and beat with electric beater or hand beater. Should be the consistency of snow. Serves 8.

Place in parfait glasses; top with a strawberry and enjoy summer elegance!

Strawberry Ice adds a Festive touch to summer living.

Great with summer fruits—strawberries, blueberries, and peaches!

Ricotta-filled Dessert Crepes

1⅛ cups flour
4½ tablespoons sugar
½ teaspoon salt
3 eggs, well beaten
1½ cups milk
1 tablespoon melted butter or oil
1½ tablespoons brandy or vanilla

In a deep bowl, sift flour, sugar, and salt. Combine eggs and milk, add to flour mixture, and stir until smooth. Add butter and brandy. Let stand overnight.

Rub a small frying pan or crepe pan with a piece of bacon fat. When pan is very hot (a drop of water should "dance" in the pan), pour a small amount of batter into pan, tilting pan so that batter covers bottom. Turn crepe gently and cook just until both sides are light brown, about 1-2 minutes. Makes 2 dozen crepes. Crepes freeze very well between layers of waxed paper.

Filling:

1 pound ricotta
8 ounces sour cream
1 teaspoon vanilla
½ cup sugar

Combine ricotta, sour cream, vanilla, and sugar. Spoon into crepes and roll each crepe. Sprinkle with powdered sugar and top with your favorite fruit.

Ricotta Sweet Puffs

2 eggs
1½ teaspoons sugar
1 teaspoon vanilla
1 cup ricotta cheese
2 teaspoons baking powder
¼ teaspoon salt
1 cup flour
Oil for deep frying
Powdered sugar

Beat eggs with sugar and vanilla. Add ricotta cheese, baking powder, and salt. Blend well. Add flour until mixture is sticky. Heat oil for deep frying. Drop batter by spoonfuls into oil; fry, turning once, until golden brown. Drain on paper towels. Sprinkle with powdered sugar and serve hot. Makes 2 dozen puffs.

Autumn

Fall foods provide festive fare, rich in color, deep in flavor. In the autumn fields, their abundance stirs the festival spirit in man.

Color runs wild on the earth, crisp scents are in the air, and foods are in their fullness. Harvest brings us reason for celebration again.

Wheat shimmers in the field; stalks of corn stand erect. The pride and pomp of abundant production cry out to be exclaimed. Fruits spill over in buckets, gathered like treasures from the earth. Color is warm and exciting. Leaves crackle, trees sigh from what they have given to the earth. Until, finally, it grows cool.

To curb the chill that touches the once-warm earth, fires and ovens are lit and the sweet scents of yeast come from the kitchen again. Breads and pizzas rising are a welcome sight, puffing in proud shapes, complimented by an abundance of butchered meat. Sausages are made.

Spices for preserving the fruits and vegetables enter the air. Hot soups bubble in the pot again. Hearty stews and

minestrones, forgotten in the heat of summer, are savored now as if they were entirely new.

Crisp and ruddy apples blend well with sharp cheese for appetizing evening snacks. Peppers are roasted and blended with ripe tomatoes. Popcorn bursts loudly on the fire and hot teas whistle again in the pot.

By the height of autumn, the ripened foods have been gathered, tasted, and preserved. It is as if one last splurge of color is splashed on the earth and dashed into boiling water; then it is locked in glass before winter wins the battle.

Before that wintry chill takes hold, man has always taken time to celebrate his triumph with nature. Pumpkins and gourds decorate the American scene, finally spilling out their contents for pies. Nuts and minced meats are all a part of the fall tradition as America begins her annual harvest gathering. The celebration of Thanksgiving is a family ritual, the favorite for many. Europeans have observed that American families make a greater effort to gather at this time than at any other. If separated, families link themselves together by eating the ritual food, the turkey.

The wide range of cultures that make up America make this festive time a blend of traditional cuisines. The proud bird forms the American core of the menu. She is browned and basted in similar fashion, but stuffed with as many different dressings as there are people who make up the land.

Oysters are a favorite in New England, where the celebration began. Variations such as our own Italian one give an interesting difference to the traditional turkey. Parmesan cheese combined with moistened bread and garlic forms a souffle in the bird that puffs and bakes—bursting with flavor when released from the cavity!

Cranberry is a colorful must on any Thanksgiving table, and gelatin and fruit salads, as well as pasta, go well with the juicy bird. Spiced pies, spumoni, and applesauce ginger cake are a proper ending to the annual feast.

Harvest spills over with foods that are not only rich and deep in tradition, but savory in taste. A reason indeed for a yearly celebration!

Mama Gaziano's Chicken Soup

1 plump chicken (2-2½ pound broiler)
½ can (16 ounce) tomatoes or fresh tomatoes, cut up
2 celery stalks, cut up
1 tablespoon salt
Pepper
Pinch of saffron
¾ pound very fine noodles
Parmesan cheese

Soups

For variety or a special, festive soup, add miniature meatballs or chunks of cheese.

Place chicken in 6-quart kettle. Cover chicken with water. Add tomatoes, and celery. Add salt and pepper to taste. Simmer 1 hour.

Remove the boiled chicken. It may be served in chicken sandwiches, or eaten warm with fresh Italian bread.

Boil noodles separately in half of broth. Add remaining broth just before serving. Sprinke soup generously with Parmesan cheese. Serves 8.

Our Minestrone

¾ cup onion, chopped
2 cloves garlic, minced
3 tablespoons olive oil
1 cup chick peas or beans
¼ cup celery, chopped
1½ cups zucchini, diced
1 cup potatoes, diced
1½ cups cabbage, coarsely chopped
1 can ripe tomatoes
8 cups boiling water
2 teaspoons salt
Dash pepper
½ teaspoon basil
1 teaspoon parsley
1 cup cooked, drained macaroni

Minestrone, or Italian vegetable soup, is a hardy version of whatever the family prefers in mixed greens and beans.

Saute onions and garlic in oil. Combine remaining ingredients except macaroni. Cook until vegetables are tender, about 1½ hours. Add macaroni. Serve hot. Serves 6-8.

A small portion of beef (1½ lbs.) or pork makes a hardier version of the soup. If meat is used, brown it in the kettle first.

Good, crusty homemade bread with this soup—a soul soothing combination.

Lentil Minestrone

¼ pound lentils
2 strips bacon, cut in small pieces
1 teaspoon salt
2 cups water
1 clove garlic, minced
½ small onion, chopped
2 tablespoons olive oil
1 small can tomatoes or 2 fresh tomatoes
½ teaspoon salt
½ teaspoon pepper
½ pound broccoli
6 cups water
½ pound macaroni or spaghetti, cut into small pieces
Parmesan cheese

Simmer lentils, bacon, and salt in 2 cups water for 1½ hours. In a small saucepan, saute garlic and onion in olive oil until onion is transparent. Add tomatoes, salt, and pepper. Simmer slowly 1 hour.

In a 3-quart saucepan, bring to a boil 6 cups salted water. Add broccoli. When water has returned to a boil, add the macaroni. Cook until macaroni is tender.

Add the tomato sauce and lentils that have been cooked ahead. Simmer another 5 minutes. Serve with grated Parmesan cheese. Serves 6-8.

Veal Meatballs for Soup

½ pound ground veal
1 egg
2 tablespoons grated Parmesan cheese
2 tablespoons bread crumbs
1 tablespoon parsley
Salt and pepper
Chicken or beef broth

Combine first six ingredients. Form into balls the size of walnuts. Place in slightly greased baking pan. Brown for 10 minutes in oven at 400°.

Bring chicken or beef broth to a brisk boil. Drop meatballs into broth. Simmer 20 minutes. Serve with Parmesan cheese. Serves 6-8.

Vegetable Soup with Red Wine

Serve hot with crusty bread.

1 small onion, chopped
1 clove garlic, minced
2 tablespoons olive oil
1 beef bone or 1 cup beef stock or boullion
2 stalks celery, chopped
2 carrots, chopped
3 potatoes, cleaned and cubed
1 cup cooked beans (navy, lentil, etc.)
½ can plum tomatoes
4 quarts water
1 cup red wine
1 cup cooked, drained vermicelli

Brown onion and garlic in olive oil. Add beef bone, vegetables, seasonings, and water. Simmer slowly for 1½ hours. Add wine and vermicelli. Cook 15 minutes. Serves 6-8.

Macaroni and Bean Soup

This inexpensive "soul soup" is a regional specialty of southern Italy, traditionally served on Friday night.

½ pound pinto, butter, lima, or dried white beans
Beef bone
1 onion, chopped
1 clove garlic, minced
Small piece salt pork (2 ounces)
1 can (1 pound) tomatoes or 4 whole tomatoes, chopped
2 tablespoons tomato paste
1 teaspoon salt
3 tablespoons parsley
Pepper to taste
½ pound macaroni of choice
Parmesan or romano cheese

Soak and cook beans, with beef bone, until tender. (If necessary, you may substitute canned white beans.) Brown onion and garlic in salt pork fat. Add tomatoes, tomato paste, and seasonings. Make a paste with flour and 2 tablespoons cold water. Add to tomatoes. Add 1 quart of water.

Combine tomato sauce and beans. Simmer 1 hour. Cook macaroni in boiling salted water; drain and add to soup. Simmer 5 more minutes. Serve with generous amounts of grated cheese. Serves 6-8.

Italian Clam Soup

1 garlic clove, minced
3 tablespoons olive oil
3 16-ounce cans tomatoes or 3 pounds fresh, peeled tomatoes
3 tablespoons parsley
½ cup white wine
2 dozen clams

Saute garlic in oil. Add tomatoes, parsley, wine, and enough water to make a thin broth. Bring to a boil. Steam clams in separate pan. Remove clam meat and add to broth. Serve hot. Serves 6-8.

Top with Parmesan cheese.

Enriched Broth

4-6 cups chicken broth
2 eggs, beaten
¼ cup Parmesan cheese, grated
2½ tablespoons parsley

Boil broth. Blend beaten eggs with cheese and parsley. Pour egg mixture into boiling broth and remove from heat immediately. DO NOT STIR. Serves 6.

For extra richness, top the bread with a slice of cheese and place ovenproof soup bowl under broiler until cheese is melted.

Holiday Onion Soup

¼ cup grated Swiss or mozzarella cheese
4 large onions
4 cups hot water
6 beef boullion cubes
3 tablespoons butter
1 teaspoon sherry
Croutons or French bread rounds

Put all ingredients except croutons into blender. Blend only 10 seconds. Pour into sauce pot. Simmer 15 minutes. Sprinkle with croutons or place a slice of French bread on top. Serves 6.

Prince or Pauper Broth

1 round slice hard Italin bread per serving
1 tablespoon butter per serving
1 tablespoon Parmesan cheese per serving
6-8 cups chicken broth
2 eggs (optional)

Fry each slice of bread in butter. Sprinkle with grated Parmesan cheese. Place in individual serving bowl. Pour hot broth over bread and serve immediately.

For a richer broth, break two eggs into broth. Stir with a long fork, allowing eggs to separate into strings.

Pastina for a Quick Recovery

Delicate flavor and texture for those who are ill. Real mothering!

8 cups chicken broth
¾ pound pastina noodles
1 egg
Grated Parmesan cheese

Bring chicken broth to a boil. Pour in pastina (tiny noodles) and simmer until tender. Break an egg into the broth, stirring well. Serve with grated cheese. Serves 6-8.

Quick Beer Bread

Breads

3 cups self-rising flour
1 tablespoon sugar
12 ounces beer
½ cup (1 stick) butter or margarine, melted

Combine flour, sugar, and beer. Pour into a greased 9" x 5" loaf pan. Bake at 350° for 25 minutes. Remove from oven. Pour the melted butter on top. Return to oven for another 25 minutes at 350°. Makes 1 loaf

Mary's Vienna Bread

2½ cups warm water
2 packages dry yeast
1 tablespoon salt
1 tablespoon butter, melted
7 cups unsifted flour
Cornmeal
1 egg white
1 tablespoon cold water

Measure warm water into large warm mixing bowl. Sprinkle or crumble in yeast, stirring well until dissolved. Add salt and melted butter. Add flour and stir until well blended. Dough will be sticky. Do not knead. Place in greased bowl, cover, and let rise in a warm place about 1 hour.

Turn dough out on lightly floured board. Divide into two equal parts. Roll each part into a rectangle, about 10" x 15". Beginning at wide side, roll up tightly toward you. Seal edges by pinching together. Place loaves on greased baking sheets and sprinkle with cornmeal. Cover, let rise in warm place until double in size (about 1 hour). With a razor, make 4 diagonal slits on top of loaf.

Bake in a hot oven (450°) for 25 minutes. Remove and brush with mixture of egg white and 1 tablespoon cold water. Return to oven for 5 minutes. Makes 2 loaves.

Rising tip: If room temperature is less than 85°, let dough rise in unheated oven with a pan of hot water on the shelf below the dough.

Mama Gaziano's Crusty Italian Bread

2 packages active dry yeast
3 cups very warm (not hot) water, divided
½ cup vegetable shortening, at room temperature
1 tablespoon salt
8 cups flour

Soften yeast in ½ cup warm water. In a very large bowl combine 2½ cups warm water with ½ cup shortening, salt, and 3 cups flour. Blend in softened yeast. Work in remaining flour. Knead until smooth and elastic, about 10 minutes. Cover and let rise in a warm place until double in size (about 1½ hours). Punch dough down in center and let rise again until double (about 1 hour).

Punch down once more. Turn out on lightly floured board, divide into two portions. Generously grease 2 loaf pans. Knead dough once more, until smooth, and place in pans. Let rise once more until double in size. Bake 50-60 minutes at 400°. Makes 2 loaves.

Briullate (Sausage Rolls)

½ of Italian bread dough recipe (see previous recipe)
Oil
Salt and pepper to taste
2 pounds homemade pork sausage

When dough rises the first time, divide into 4 parts. Roll out on floured board to about ½ inch thickness. Brush with oil. Sprinkle with a little salt and pepper. Dot with small pieces of sausage (approximately ½ pound for each sausage roll).

Roll up like a jelly roll; seal the sides and twist slightly. Press the ends, gently forming the roll into the shape of a small round loaf of bread. Cover with a tea towel or plastic wrap. Let rise again. Bake 45-50 minutes at 400° Makes four sausage rolls.

*Briullate and Salads —
a hearty meal in itself.*

My sister Regina spent her teen years as pizza queen of the class, combining every conceivable Italian delicacy—peppers, pepperoni, two cheeses, mushrooms—to the delight of the ravenous team and the cheering squad.

Regina's Party Pizza

Fritta Bread Dough recipe (see page 28)
Olive oil
Basic tomato sauce (see page 24)
Oregano
Parmesan cheese
Other ingredients to taste

Let the dough rise once. Grease 4 pizza pans generously with vegetable oil. Divide the dough into 4 parts, and spread each in a pan.

Spread olive oil over dough so it will not dry out. Let rise again in warm place.

Spoon basic tomato sauce on top and sprinkle with oregano and Parmesan cheese. Add other ingredients according to your taste.

When the pizza has risen in the pan, bake 15-20 minutes at 425°, until crust is light brown. To make a moister pizza, I remove the pizzas from the oven after 15 minutes, add more sauce and mozzarella cheese so that the cheese will melt but not burn. At that point the party can begin!

Variations:

A meatless favorite for us is the combination of anchovies and mushrooms. Teenages enjoy thinly sliced pepperoni and mozzarella cheese. Pizza shells may be prepared and frozen, saving the last step for a group to do together.

Calabrian Fritta dough in many forms: wrapped around fish; in pizza, for baked rolls, and sweet rolls.

Meats and Meat Dishes

Helen's Hearty Chicken Cacciatore

1 large cut up fryer
¼ cup olive oil
1 onion, cut up
1 clove garlic, minced
1 large can tomatoes (or 3 whole tomatoes, peeled)
1 small can tomato paste (6 ounces)
1 green pepper, sliced
1 teaspoon salt
½ teaspoon pepper
1 teaspoon oregano
1 teaspoon basil
1 pound fresh mushrooms (sliced)
1 cup red wine

Brown the fryer in olive oil. Add onion and garlic as chicken browns. Add tomatoes and tomato paste, with enough water to make a thin sauce. Add pepper and seasonings. Cover; let simmer 45 minutes or until chicken is tender. Add mushrooms and wine. Cook 15 minutes more. Serves 6.

Hot Pot and Cabbage

A hearty entree for chilly winter nights.

3 pounds cubed beef
3 tablespoons flour
6-8 potatoes, peeled
1 cup chopped celery
2 onions, chopped
2 carrots, chopped
1 cup boullion
1 head red cabbage, shredded
2 apples, peeled and sliced
2 tablespoons vinegar
2 tablespoons sugar

Butter a deep casserole. Dredge beef in flour. Layer beef in casserole with cubed potatoes, celery, onions, and carrots, reserving one potato. Pour 1 cup boullion over all.

Slice the last potato thinly and arrange the slices as a crust for the hot pot. Cover with foil or a lid and bake 1 hour at 350°. Remove cover. Cook uncovered for ½ hour longer to allow the potato crust to brown. Add more boullion if necessary.

While the casserole cooks, boil the red cabbage and apples. Cook until the cabbage is tender. Drain well. Combine the vinegar and sugar. Toss over cabbage and refrigerate.

Serve the hot pot steaming hot with the chilled red cabbage spooned on top. Serves 6-8.

Pork, Peaches, and Yellow Rice

3 packages yellow rice (6-ounce package)
1 can beer (12 ounces)
4 cups chicken broth or boullion
½ medium onion, chopped
1 green pepper, chopped
5-6 pork chops
1 can peach halves

Butter a large casserole. Combine the rice, beer, and chicken broth in casserole. Saute onion and green pepper, and add to casserole. Cover and let bake at 325° for 1 hour. While the rice cooks, broil 5-6 plump pork chops, browning but not drying the meat. Take the casserole from the oven (the liquid should be absorbed). Arrange pork chops and peaches on top. Add a touch of green pepper or parsley for color and return to the oven for ½ hour more. Serves 6.

Stuffed Peppers or Zucchini

6 green peppers or 6 medium zucchini
2 cups Italian bread, softened in cold water
2 pounds ground beef (or 1 pound beef and 1 pound pork)
½ cup grated Parmesan cheese
1 tablespoon parsley
1 teaspoon salt

Dash pepper

1 small onion, minced
1 clove garlic, finely minced
4 eggs
Basic tomato sauce (see page 24)

Prepare bread by soaking in COLD water (hot water will make it gummy). After it is thoroughly soaked, squeeze out the water. Mix bread well with remaining ingredients.

If you use zucchini, you may use some of the pulp in place of some of the bread. Zucchini may be stuffed lengthwise.

Cut peppers in half and remove seeds and pulp. Stuff peppers and place in a baking dish. Pour tomato sauce over the peppers. Bake 1 hour at 350°. Serves 12.

Mediterranean Paella

1 large green pepper
2 large onions, chopped
2 cloves garlic, minced
Olive oil
1 pinch saffron
1 can beer
1 cup vermouth
1 small jar green pimento-stuffed olives
1 small can tomato sauce
3 chicken thighs
3 pork chops
6 fresh clams
1 pound yellow rice
1 small can peas for garnish
(squid, shrimp, mussels optional)

Saute green peppers, onion, and garlic in olive oil. Add crushed saffron. Brown chicken and pork in oil. Bone and cube chicken and pork.

In a greased casserole, combine all ingredients except peas. Bake 45 minutes at 400°. Decorate with peas and more pimentos. If the rice seems dry, add chicken broth.

Paella may be simple and delectable with chicken and pork, or elaborate and exciting with a fisherman's catch of exotic seafood. A superb touch that will delight even the most highly regarded guest includes squid tentacles and rings, clams, mussels, and jumbo shrimp with the pink tails artistically swirled outward. These delicacies should be boiled, cleaned, and readied while the rice cooks. After they are added to the dish, it should be covered and reheated for 10 minutes more.

The beauty of this and many relatively simple dishes is in the artistic arrangement of ingredients in appealing design. Here is where the artist fits into the kitchen—combining color, texture, and taste.

Choice vegetables, marinated, baked in Paella, stuffed in zucchini.

For a holiday breakfast platter, fill this ring with hot scrambled eggs.

Holiday Sausage Ring

2 pounds ground sausage
2 eggs
1½ cups cracker crumbs
¼ cup minced onions
1 cup diced apple

Mix all ingredients and mold into a ring. Bake 1 hour at 350°. Decorate with parsley. Serves 6-8.

Add ½ ounce crushed red pepper if you prefer hot sausage.

Mild Italian Sausage

8 pounds coarsely ground pork (a Boston butt is a good cut)
¾ ounce black pepper
1¾ ounces salt
¼ ounce fennel
1 pound cleaned hog casings

The making of sausage is a family or communal ritual, requiring several hands. Mix the first five ingredients well, by hand, and stuff into hog casings.

There are many ways to enjoy sausage. For a delicate variety, wrap the sausages in waxed paper and toss under coals to roast. It is also good cut and placed on a skewer, brushed with a little of your favorite barbecue sauce. "Pig in pastry" offers variety to bread dough. And sandwiches of sausage and fried green peppers are yet another delightful use for flavorful pork.

Intimate Italian Brunch, Sausage, Pitta Rolls and Coffee.

Sausage, Tomatoes, and Potatoes

Great for after the game.

1 pound Italian sausage
5 medium potatoes, sliced
1 medium onion, chopped
1 green pepper, chopped
1 teaspoon salt
Pepper to taste
2 cups basic tomato sauce (see page 24)

Brown sausage, potatoes, onion, and pepper separately. Drain all excess grease. Add seasonings and sauce. Let simmer for a while before serving. Serves 6-8.

Sausage, Potatoes, and Eggs

1 pound Italian sausage
Oil for frying
5 medium potatoes
5 eggs, well beaten
1 teaspoon salt
Pepper to taste

Brown sausage under broiler or in large skillet. Drain all excess grease. Slice potatoes coarsely and fry until golden brown. Drain excess oil. Combine sausage and potatoes. Pour eggs over, and toss gently over heat, just until eggs are cooked. Serves 6.

Sausage and Egg Ring

1 pound ground pork sausage
6 eggs, beaten
2 cups milk
6 slices bread
1 cup grated sharp cheddar cheese
1 teaspoon mustard
Dash salt

Brown, drain, and cool sausage. Mix the eggs, milk, bread, cheese, mustard, and salt. Add sausage. Place in a well greased ring mold. Refrigerate overnight. Bake 45 minutes at 350°. Unmold, fill with scrambled eggs, and garnish with parsley for a holiday brunch. Serves 6-8.

Veal Sweetened with Marsala

1½ pounds veal cutlets
Flour
1 teaspoon salt
Pepper to taste
4 tablespoons butter
1 cup Marsala wine
Juice of 1 lemon

Dip cutlets in flour. Season with salt and pepper. Brown gently in butter. Add Marsala and lemon juice, blend, and serve. Serves 3-4.

Italian Pork Roast

Pork roast (3-4 pounds)
¼ cup olive oil
2 tablespoons butter
1 clove garlic, cut into slivers
1 tablespoon rosemary
1 tablespoon thyme
1 teaspoon salt
Dash of pepper

Rub roast with oil, melted butter, and garlic. Make a few slits in the roast and embed the garlic slivers. Sprinkle on the other seasonings.

Bake at 400° for ½ hour, then reduce heat to 325° until done, cooking approximately 25 minutes per pound and basting frequently.

During the last 15 minutes of cooking, drain off excess grease and add 1 can apricots or baked apples. Remove to a hot platter. Garnish with fruit and serve warm. Serves 6.

Sirloin Rolled Roast

1½-pound top sirloin
1½-pound bottom sirloin
1 tablespoon parsley
1 clove garlic, minced
1 teaspoon thyme
Salt and pepper to taste
1 teaspoon rosemary

Place fat sides together. Spread herbs between two steaks. Roll together like a jelly roll. Tie with string. Bake 20 minutes per pound at 350°. Serves 6.

Liver and Onions, Italian Style

2 tablespoons butter
½ cup olive oil
2 pounds liver
4 large onions
Juice of 1 lemon
1 teaspoon salt
Pepper to taste
Parsley
¼ cup white wine

Heat oil and butter. Saute liver and onions until golden brown. Add lemon juice, salt, pepper, parsley, and wine. Let simmer 10-15 minutes. Serves 6-8.

Turkey in Brown Bag

For a truly moist, brown bird, try a large grocery bag! Gently place a stuffed, buttered turkey in a large, brown bag. Secure ends, leaving enough space for air to circulate. Place in a roasting pan and let it bake! The juices stay in—tender, brown, moist meat is the result.

Tripe with Tomatoes

1 whole onion
½ pound stewing beef
3 tablespoons olive oil
3 pounds tripe
1 can tomatoes or 2 whole tomatoes
2 tablespoons tomato paste
1 teaspoon salt
Dried red pepper to taste
Parsley

To some a delicacy, to others a practical use of every part of meat. Used well and with a little care, tripe can be savory.

Brown onion and stewing beef in olive oil. While it is browning, boil tripe separately until tender. Combine drained tripe and browned beef and onions in a pot, adding enough water to cover. Add tomatoes and tomato paste. Season with crushed red pepper, salt, and parsley. Simmer ½ hour. Serves 6-8.

Stuffed Veal Breast

3-pound veal breast
1½ pounds ground round
1½ cups Italian bread, softened in cold water
1½ cups grated Parmesan cheese
1 tablespoon parsley
1½ teaspoons salt
1 clove garlic, minced
Dash black pepper
3 eggs

Have butcher make a slit pocket in veal breast. Combine remaining ingredients, and mix well. Stuff into pocket. Rub salt and pepper over breast. Bake 25 minutes per pound at 350°. Serves 6.

Beautiful with roasted apples.

Stuffed Pork Chops

6 thick pork chops
1 cup bread crumbs
1 egg
½ cup Parmesan cheese, grated
1 tablespoon parsley
1 teaspoon salt
1 teaspoon pepper

Have butcher prepare a slit pocket in thick, lean pork chops. Brown pork chops on both sides. Combine remaining ingredients, mix well, and place stuffing in pockets. Secure with toothpicks. Place in a dutch oven or roasting pan. Bake 1½ hours at 350°. Serves 6.

Tenderized steak may be used in place of veal.

Grandma's Homecoming Veal

6 veal cutlets, ½ inch thick
Salt and pepper to taste
2-3 eggs, slightly beaten with 2 tablespoons milk

Breading:

½ cup Parmesan cheese, grated
1 cup fine bread crumbs
1 tablespoon chopped parsley
1 small clove garlic, finely chopped
½ teaspoon salt

Season cutlets with salt and pepper. Mix together the breading ingredients. Dip the cutlets first in the egg mixture and then in the breading mixture. Saute in hot grease until well browned. Serves 6.

Veal with Provolone

A slightly different flavor for an old Italian favorite.

2 pounds veal cutlets
4 tablespoons butter or margarine
½ cup white wine
½ teaspoon fresh basil
1 teaspoon salt
1 teaspoon pepper
6 slices provolone cheese

Brown veal in butter. Add wine and seasonings, and simmer slowly for 15 minutes. Remove veal and place in ovenproof dish or metal platter. Pour cooked wine sauce over cutlets. Top each cutlet with a slice of provolone cheese. Bake in a hot oven 425° 5-10 minutes or put under broiler 2-3 minutes, until cheese melts. Serves 4.

Italian Oven Baked Chicken

My Aunt Mary guarantees it will melt in your mouth!

¾ cup butter or margarine (1½ sticks)
1 fryer, cut up
3 tablespoons flour
1 teaspoon salt
Pepper to taste
1 tablespoon oregano

Melt butter in a heavy skillet. Dredge chicken in flour and place in skillet. Season with salt, pepper, and oregano. Brown chicken on both sides, then remove from pan. Place chicken and butter in a shallow roasting pan. Bake at 350° for 45 minutes. Serves 6.

Chicken Gizzards, Italian Style

2 pounds chicken gizzards (cut up)
¼ cup oil
¼ cup margarine
1 large onion, chopped
4 green peppers, cut up
1 cup tomato sauce
1 teaspoon salt
½ teaspoon garlic powder
1 teaspoon mixed Italian spices
½ teaspoon pepper

Parboil gizzards until tender. Combine oil and margarine in frying pan. Add gizzards, onion, and green peppers; cook for a few minutes. Add remaining ingredients and simmer for 30 minutes, uncovered. Serves 6-8.

Roasted Peppers

6 green or red sweet peppers
1 clove garlic, minced
3 tablespoons olive oil
1 teaspoon crushed red pepper

Place green peppers on greased cookie sheet. Bake at 350° for 1 hour or until browned. When cool, skin pepper. (Skin will pull off easily after roasting.) Remove seeds and cut pepper in strips. Season with remaining ingredients.

Quick Fried Rice

4 tablespoons butter or margarine
1 teaspoon salt
1 cup rice
1¾ cup hot boullion or chicken broth

Melt butter in a skillet. Add salt, Add uncooked rice and saute over medium heat until rice is opaque. Put in an oven-proof dish. Add the heated boullion or broth. Bake 20-30 minutes, uncovered, at 325°. Garnish with shrimp, cooked pork, or thin strips of fried egg. Serves 4.

As an appetizer, the lovely flowerette adds interest to a table setting.

Dom's Artichokes

4 artichokes
1 cup grated cheese
1 cup dry bread crumbs
1 teaspoon salt
½ teaspoon garlic
1 tablespoon parlsey
4 teaspoons olive oil

Clean artichokes. Remove stem. Mix together remaining ingredients. Stuff cheese mixture between leaves of artichokes. Pour 1 teaspoon olive oil on each artichoke. Place in heavy saucepan. Add a little water, enough to steam the vegetables. Close lid tightly and steam for 45 minutes. Serves 4.

Zucchini Torte

6 cups zucchini, diced
1½ cups Bisquick
1½ cups Cheddar cheese, grated
½ cup oil
4 eggs, beaten
1 onion, chopped
Salt and pepper to taste

Mix all ingredients. Spread in an ungreased 9" x 12" pan. Bake 35-40 minutes at 350°. Serve in squares. Serves 8.

Mushrooms Parmesan

1 pound fresh mushrooms
4 tablespoons olive oil
1 teaspoon chopped parsley
3 tablespoon bread crumbs
4 tablespoons grated Parmesan cheese

Clean mushrooms and place in baking dish. Drizzle olive oil over mushrooms. Sprinkle with parsley, bread crumbs, and cheese. Bake 15 minutes at 350°. Serves 6-8.

Pan Roasted Potatoes

Country elegance—the simple flavor of pan roasted potatoes is different from oven roasted.

6 large potatoes or 12 new potatoes
½ cup butter
1 tablespoon fresh parsley
1 teaspoon salt
Dash freshly ground pepper

Parboil potatoes with jackets on until firm and tender, but not completely soft. Drain. Cool under running cold water; remove peels. Cut large potatoes into halves or quarters; leave small new potatoes whole.

Melt butter in large, heavy skillet. Pat potatoes dry and place in warmed butter. Sprinkle with parsley, salt, and pepper. Keep turning, over heat, until potatoes are golden brown. Serves 6.

Flank Steak Roll

4 6-inch strips of flank steak
½ loaf hardened Italian bread
½ cup grated Parmesan cheese
1 tablespoon parsley
1 teaspoon salt
½ teaspoon pepper
2 eggs
1 clove garlic, minced

Sauce:

1 clove garlic, minced
1 small onion, chopped
Olive oil
1 can plum tomatoes (16 ounces)
1 small can tomato paste (6 ounces)

Have butcher prepare steak. Brown gently in butter. To make the stuffing, soak hard bread in cold water, then squeeze water out. Combine bread with cheese, parsley, salt, pepper, eggs, and garlic. Mix well. Spread stuffing on flattened meat. Roll up like a jelly roll. Tie together with string.

To make sauce, saute the minced garlic clove and chopped onion in olive oil. Add tomatoes, tomato paste, and enough water to make a thin sauce. Simmer 30 minutes. Add rolled meat. Cook slowly in pot or baking casserole for 1 hour. Serves 6-8.

This stuffing is equally good in roasted chickens.

Parmesan Dressing for Turkey

For a 12-15 pound turkey:

4 cups Italian bread
1 clove garlic, minced
1 onion, chopped finely
2 tablespoons parsley
4 eggs
1 teaspoon salt
Pepper
¾ cup grated Parmesan cheese
3-4 tablespoons chopped celery
Chopped gizzard from turkey

Soak the bread in cold water, then squeeze water out. Combine bread with remaining ingredients; mix well with hands. Stuff bird. Any leftover stuffing can be baked in a small oven casserole. Stuffing should puff like a souffle as the turkey browns.

Sweet and Sour Autumn Pork

Serve with fried rice.

1½ pounds pork, cut into strips
1 medium green pepper, cut into strips
2 medium onions, thinly sliced
½ cup water
⅓ cup vinegar
½ cup brown sugar
2 tablespoons cornstarch
½ teaspoon salt
1 can pineapple chunks (20 ounce can) with juice

Brown pork in large electic skillet. Saute pepper and onions until tender.

In a small saucepan, combine water, vinegar, sugar, cornstarch, salt, pineapple, and 1 cup pineapple juice. Cook until sauce is clear and thickened. Pour the sauce over meat and vegetables. Cover and cook on low heat 30 minutes. Serves 4.

Subtle Venetian Spareribs

4 pounds spareribs
2 tablespoons cornstarch
1 teaspoon Accent
⅔ cup soy sauce
⅔ cup firmly packed light brown sugar
¼ cup cider vinegar
⅓ cup finely chopped crystallized ginger
2 cloves garlic, minced

Cut spareribs into serving sized pieces and put into a large saucepan. Add enough water to cover. Cover pot and bring to a boil. Reduce heat and simmer 2 hours.

For the sauce, blend the cornstarch, Accent, and soy sauce, then mix in the remaining ingredients. Drain spareribs and drop each piece into the sauce, coating well.

Transfer spareribs to a broiler rack. Broil, with tops of ribs about 3 inches from heat, about 5 minutes or until richly browned, brushing two or three times with the sauce. Turn ribs and brush generously with sauce. Broil second side until richly browned, about 3 minutes, brushing once or twice with sauce. Serves 8.

Vegetables &
Side Dishes

Zucchini Provolone Bake

1 pound unpeeled zucchini
Flour
½ cup oil
2 green peppers
½ pround provolone cheese, shredded
½ cup grated Parmesan cheese
1 teaspoon salt
Dash pepper
1 teaspoon parsley
1 teaspoon basil
½ cup bread crumbs

Wash, but do not peel, zucchini. Slice in ¼-inch pieces. Dip each piece in flour and brown in oil. Set aside zucchini. Cut up peppers and saute in remaining oil. In a 2-quart casserole, alternate layers of zucchini and peppers with cheeses, seasonings, and bread crumbs, ending with bread crumbs. Bake at 350° for 45 minutes. Serves 6-8.

Broiled Zucchini and Anchovy Boats

4 whole zucchini
3 tablespoons butter
1 clove garlic, minced
2 tablespoons olive oil
1 can anchovy fillets
1 tablespoon parsley
¾ cup fine bread crumbs, divided

Boil whole zucchini until tender but not mushy, about 15 minutes. Drain and cool under cold running water. Dry and cut lengthwise. Place zucchini halves in baking dish. With a knife, make crisscross slits in zucchini pulp. Insert dots of butter in slits.

Brown garlic in olive oil. Add the anchovies, parsley, and ½ cup bread crumbs to oil. Mix and brown the mixture over low heat for just 2-3 minutes. Distribute over zucchini. Top with remaining ¼ cup bread crumbs. Broil 5 minutes. Serves 6-8.

Peppers and Tomatoes for Now and Later

Delicious in omelettes, on ham sandwiches, or on a buffet table with cheese and fresh bread.

1 clove garlic
3 tablespoons olive oil
1 large onion
10 tomatoes
10 sweet peppers
1 teaspoon salt
Dash pepper
1 can tomato paste

In late summer, when peppers and tomatoes are ripe and inexpensive, this lovely combination can be easily prepared. Store by canning in sterile jars or freeze in plastic freezer containers.

Brown garlic in oil. Add one large onion. Wash and core tomatoes and peppers. Add tomatoes, pepper, salt, pepper, and tomato paste. Simmer 1 hour in a large saucepan. Cool.

Crustless Vegetable Pie

1 eggplant, peeled and cubed
2 medium zucchini, cubed
1 large onion, chopped
¼ cup oil
4 tomatoes, peeled and chopped
½ pound mushrooms, sliced
3 eggs
¾ cup grated Parmesan cheese, divided
1 tablespoon parsley
½ teaspoon basil
½ teaspoon oregano
Salt and pepper to taste
¼ pound mozzarella cheese

Saute eggplant, zucchini, and onion in oil for about 10 minutes. Add tomatoes, cover, and simmer for 20 minutes. Add mushrooms.

Beat eggs with ¼ cup Parmesan cheese, parsley, basil, and oregano. Add to vegetables. Pour half the mixture into a greased 9" pie plate. Top with ¼ cup Parmesan cheese.

Layer with remaining vegetables and ¼ cup Parmesan cheese. Top with mozzarella cheese. Bake, uncovered, 40-45 minutes at 350°, or until set and browned on top. Serves 8-10.

Toasted Carrots

1 pound medium carrots
½ cup water
1 teaspoon sugar
½ teaspoon salt
¼ cup melted butter
1 cup crushed corn flakes

Clean the carrots and, if large, cut in half lengthwise and crosswise. Put in a saucepan with water, sugar, and salt. Cover and cook until tender, about 15 minutes. Roll the cooked carrots in melted butter, then in crushed corn flakes. Place in a shallow baking dish. Bake at 350° for 15 minutes. Serves 4.

Rice Croquettes

3 cups cold cooked rice (refrigerated at least one day)
2 eggs
½ cup grated Parmesan or cubed mozzarella cheese
1 tablespoon parsley
Salt and pepper to taste
1 egg beaten
½ cup bread crumbs

Mix together the rice, 2 eggs, cheese, parsley, salt and pepper. Roll into balls the size of a golf ball. Dip balls in beaten egg, then in bread crumbs. Fry in hot oil. Serve hot. Serves 6-8.

A mellow variation: Omit the tomatoes. Layer fried eggplant with Parmesan cheese, top with mozzarella, and bake as above.

Baked Eggplant

2 large eggplants
Salt
Flour
Oil or butter
2 cans plum tomatoes (16 ounces)
½ cup grated Parmesan cheese
1 pound mozzarella cheese

Slice eggplants in half lengthwise. Remove eggplant pulp from shell and cut into slices. Salt slice pulp in bowl. Set aside for 1 hour.

Dip each piece in flour and fry in butter or olive oil. In a baking dish, alternate layers of fried eggplant with canned tomatoes and Parmesan cheese. Top with mozzarella. Bake uncovered for ½ hour at 350°. Serves 4.

Hot Cherry Tomatoes

An artful decoration around roast or fish.

About 40 miniature tomatoes
1 cup bread crumbs, softened in cold water, squeezed
2 onions, chopped
4 tablespoons parsley
Salt and pepper to taste
1 clove garlic, minced
Oil or butter

Remove half the pulp from the tomatoes. Place the tomatoes in a baking dish. Make a stuffing of the bread, onions, parsley, salt, pepper, and garlic. Stuff tomatoes. Sprinkle olive oil or melted butter over the top. Bake 10-15 minutes at 375°.

Baked Squash and Egg Squares

4 cups zucchini or other summer squash (2 pounds)
3 eggs
⅔ cup grated Parmesan or Romano cheese, or a mixture of both
3 tablespoons melted butter or olive oil
1 teaspoon salt
2 tablespoons cracker meal

Clean, peel, and grate squash. Add other ingredients and mix thoroughly. Spoon into a greased 9" x 13" baking dish. Bake, uncovered, 1 hour at 325°. Cut into squares. Serves 8.

Quick Fry Mushrooms and Carrots

1 pound carrots
1 pound mushrooms
3 tablespoons oil

Sauce:

3 tablespoons sugar
3 tablespoons soy sauce
1 teaspoon Accent

Slice carrots in diagonal slivers; cut mushrooms lengthwise. Fry quickly, turning often, in oil. Prepare sauce by mixing, in a small saucepan, the sugar, soy sauce, and Accent. Heat sauce and pour over drained vegetables. Serves 6-8.

Hot Sandwiches and Such

Fried Italian Bread and Cheese Sandwiches

1 loaf Italian bread
2 pounds mozzarella or provolone cheese
3 eggs, well beaten

Cut Italian loaf into sandwich rounds. Cut the crust off, and use it to make fine bread crumbs (grate the crusts on a cheese grater or use a food processor).

Insert cheese slices between two pieces of bread. Dip the sandwiches into egg, then into bread crumbs. Fry in hot fat.

Peasant's Pride

Crusty homemade bread
Chunks of provolone or Parmesan cheese
Green olives

The meal that fortified the peasant may please the most epicurean palate. Before entering the sulfur mines of Sicily, miners dined on the simple combination of good olives, cheese, and bread. The perfection of this dish is in the freshness of homemade bread, the richness of the olives, and the mellowness of aged cheeses.

Italian Fondue

1 teaspoon cornstarch
⅓ cup milk
1½ pounds fontina or mozzarella cheese, cubed
½ teaspoon salt
½ teaspoon white pepper
4 egg yolks
6 slices Italian bread, toasted and cut into cubes

Combine cornstarch and milk, stirring until cornstarch is completely dissolved. In a saucepan, combine the cornstarch and milk, cheese, salt, and pepper. Cook over low heat, stirring, until cheese is melted and all ingredients are blended. Beat egg yolks. Gently add egg yolks to cheese mixture, over very low heat, stirring constantly. Let the mixture thicken, watching carefully. Put the fondue in a warming dish or small individual bowls. Dip toasted bread into sauce. Serves 6.

Italian Chile for Hot Dogs

1 pound ground round
1 clove garlic, minced
2 onions, minced
2 tablespoons oil
1 teaspoon crushed red pepper
3 tablespoons chili powder
1 can tomato paste

Brown the beef, garlic, and onion in oil. Add the seasonings and tomato paste, and enough water to make a thin sauce. Simmer, uncovered, for 30 minutes, or until sauce is thickened.

Hot Sausage and Pepper Sandwiches

French or Italian bread
Italian sausage
Green peppers
Olive oil

Variation: Simmer the sausage and peppers in tomato sauce, heap onto bread.

Slit one long loaf of French or Italian bread lengthwise, or use small individual loaves.

Broil sausage; fry peppers in olive oil. Combine and generously fill bread loaf. Serve warm.

Skewered Bread and Cheese

1 pound provolone or mozzarella cheese, cut in cubes
1 loaf Italian bread, cut in cubes
Green peppers (optional)
½ cup butter (1 stick)
1 can anchovies (2 ounces)

Alternate cheese, bread, and pepper slices on skewers.

Combine butter and anchovies in a small saucepan. Heat, gently stirring, until well blended.

Broil the skewered ingredients, basting with the butter sauce. Serves 6-8.

Toasted Loaf of Bread and Cheese

1 stick butter
⅓ cup Romano cheese
¼ cup Parmesan cheese
1 teaspoon paprika
1 loaf crusty homemade bread
2 6-ounce packages mozzarella cheese
Garlic powder

Melt butter. Add Romano and Parmesan cheeses and paprika. Blend well. Cut the loaf of bread in half lengthwise and spread with butter and cheese mixture. Sprinkle on mozzarella cheese and garlic powder. Broil until light brown, watching carefully. Cut into individual pieces and serve hot.

Hoagies

4 8-inch rolls
2 large onions
2 green peppers
½ cup butter (1 stick)
2 pounds sandwich steak
1 pound mozzarella cheese

Slit rolls lengthwise. Saute onions and peppers in butter. Set aside. Brown steak in butter. Place peppers, onions, and steak generously in rolls. Top with mozzarella cheese. Wrap tightly with aluminum foil. Heat in oven 10-15 minutes at 400°. Serves 4.

Italian Hamburgers

2 pounds ground round
1 pound fresh mushrooms
4 tablespoons butter
1 pound mozzarella cheese
Italian rolls

Form ground beef into patties. Put in broiler pan and broil on one side. Turn patty and brown lightly. In a skillet, saute mushrooms in butter. Just before the hamburgers are browned on the second side, place a piece of mozzarella cheese on each patty. Top with mushrooms. Return to the broiler just until cheese melts. Serve on crusty Italian rolls. Makes about 10 sandwiches.

Zucchini Bread

5 eggs
2 cups sugar
1 cup oil
2 cups zucchini, peeled and chopped
2 cups flour
¼ teaspoon baking powder
2 teaspoons baking soda
1 teaspoon salt
1 teaspoon cinnamon
1 teaspoon vanilla or rum
½ cup raisins
½ cup nuts, chopped

Combine eggs, sugar, and oil. Add zucchini. Sift together dry ingredients and add to mixture. Add vanilla, raisins, and nuts. Mix well and pour into loaf pans. Bake 40 minutes at 350°. Makes two loaves.

Applesauce Fruitcake

Variation: Use loaf pans for smaller cakes. Bake only about 2 hours.

3 cups applesauce
1 cup shortening
2 cups sugar
1 pound pitted dates, chopped
1 pound light or dark raisins
½ pound candied cherries, quarterd
½ pound candied pineapple, chopped
½ pound citron, finely chopped
1 pound nuts, coarsely chopped
4½ cups sifted flour
4 teaspoons baking soda
1 teaspoon nutmeg
2½ teaspoons ground cinnamon
½ teaspoon ground cloves
1 teaspoon salt

Boil applesauce, shortening, and sugar together for 5 minutes, stirring occasionally. Let stand until cool.

Mix the dates, raisins, candied fruits, citron, and nuts together in a large (3 quart) mixing bowl. Sift together the flour, soda, spices, and salt over the fruit until each piece of fruit is coated.

Stir in the cooled applesauce mixture. Turn into a large tube pan. Place a pan of water on the lower shelf of your oven. Bake the fruitcake at 250° until a straw comes out clean, about 4 hours. Makes a 7-8 pound cake.

Applesauce Cake

1 cup shortening
2 cups sugar
2 eggs, beaten
2 cups applesauce
1 teaspoon salt
2 teaspoons cinnamon
2 teaspoons nutmeg
2 teaspoons cloves
1 teaspoon allspice
2 teaspoons soda
4 tablespoons hot water
1 cup chopped nuts
1 cup raisins
 4 cups flour

Thoroughly cream shortening and sugar; add eggs and beat well. Add applesauce. Sift together and add all dry ingredients except soda. Dissolve soda in hot water, stir into batter. Beat until smooth. Fold in raisins and nuts. Bake 60 minutes at 350° in a well-greased tube pan.

Italian Coffee Cake

1 cup butter (2 sticks)
1¼ cups sugar
2 eggs
1 teaspoon vanilla
1 cup sour cream
2 cups flour
1 teaspoon baking powder
1 teaspoon salt
1 teaspoon baking soda
½ cup pecans or walnuts, ground
¼ cup sugar
1 teaspoon cinnamon

Cream the butter and 1¼ cups sugar. Add eggs, beating well. Add vanilla and sour cream. Sift together flour, baking powder, salt, and soda. Add to creamed mixture. Pour half the batter in a greased and floured pan. Mix the ground nuts, ¼ cup sugar, and cinnamon. Spread half the nut mixture over batter in pan. Pour in the rest of the batter. Top with remaining nut mixture. Bake 50-60 minutes at 350°.

Sharon's Coffee Cake

⅓ cup sugar
¼ cup butter
1 egg
½ teaspoon shredded lemon peel
½ teaspoon vanilla
¾ cup flour
1 teaspoon baking powder
¼ teaspoon salt
3 tablespoons milk
¼ cup brown sugar
¼ teaspoon cinnamon
2 tablespoons butter
2 tablespoons chopped walnuts

West Virginia's First Lady, Sharon Rockefeller adds a touch of autumn hospitality to our gathered recipes.

Thoroughly cream sugar and ¼ cup butter. Beat in egg, lemon peel, and vanilla. Stir together ¾ cup flour, baking powder, and salt; add alternately with milk. Turn into a greased and floured 6½" x 6½" x 2" baking dish.

Combine brown sugar, ¼ cup flour, and cinnamon; cut in 2 tablespoons butter until crumbly. Stir in walnuts. Sprinkle brown sugar mixture over batter in pans. Bake 30 minutes at 350°.

Black Raspberry Cake

1 cup shortening
2 cups granulated sugar
3 eggs, separated
1 cup sour milk or buttermilk
1 teaspoon vanilla
3 cups cake flour
½ teaspoon salt
1 teaspoon baking soda
1 teaspoon cinnamon
½ teaspoon baking powder
1 cup black raspberries, drained

Cream shortening and sugar. Add egg yolks and milk; blend thoroughly. Add vanilla, flour, salt, baking soda, and cinnamon; mix well. Beat egg whites with ½ teaspoon baking powder; fold into batter. Gently fold in raspberries. Bake in a greased 10-inch tube pan 30-35 minutes at 350°.

Serve plain or with strawberry topping.

Ricotta Cheesecake

Crust:

1½ cups zwieback, crushed
3 tablespoons sugar
¼ cup butter
Dash cinnamon

Filling:

2 8-ounce packages cream cheese
1 pound ricotta cheese
1½ cups sugar
4 eggs, slightly beaten
3 rounded tablespoons flour
1½ tablespoons lemon juice
2 tablespoons vanilla
½ cup margarine or butter
1 pint sour cream

Mix together crust ingredients and press into bottom of large spring-form pan.

Cream together the cream cheese, ricotta cheese, sugar, and eggs. Add the flour, lemon juice, vanilla, butter, and sour cream. (If using an electric mixer, turn to low speed to add flour and remaining ingredients.) Pour onto crust in spring-form pan. Bake at 325° for 1 hour and 10 minutes. Turn off oven, and let cake stand in oven 2 hours after oven is turned off. Refrigerate for 24 hours.

Strawberry Topping for Cheesecake

2 pints firm strawberries
¾ cup red currant jelly

Clean and hull strawberries. Heat currant jelly, stirring, until it melts. Cool jelly for 5 minutes.

Arrange strawberries on cheesecake. Pour glaze over berries.

Stuffed Flamed Peaches

An exotic dessert that is simple to prepare—a spectacle to watch and a joy to eat!

6 peaches
1 cup crushed macaroons
⅓ cup almonds, finely chopped
3 tablespoons lemon rind, grated
3 tablespoons melted butter
6 tablespoons sugar
6 tablespoons Marsala wine (sherry can be used)
Kirsch or rum

Cut peaches in half, remove pits. Combine macaroons, almonds, grated lemon rind, butter, and sugar. Fill each peach half with the mixture. Pour ½ tablespoon Marsala over each peach half. Bake until tender (about 25 minutes) at 350°.

Place the peaches in a chafing dish. Pour warm kirsch or rum over the peaches and light. Serves 6.

Date Nut Ice Cream Cake

Serve with or without orange sauce—a holiday delight!

¾ cup butter
2½ cups sugar
6 eggs
3½ cups flour
1 teaspoon salt
1 teaspoon soda
½ cup Karo syrup
½ cup white wine
1 16-ounce package dates, chopped
1 pound pecans, coarsely chopped
½ cup flour

Cream butter and sugar until light and fluffy. Add eggs one at a time, beating well after each addition. Sift together flour, salt, and soda. Add alternately with Karo syrup and wine. Dredge dates and nuts in ½ cup flour; fold into batter. Pour batter into a large greased tube pan. Put a pan of hot water under the cake, on the lower oven rack. Bake 3 hours at 275°.

When cake is cooled, slit in two layers. Put vanilla ice cream between layers. Freeze. Serve in 1-inch slices.

Italian Cream Cake

1 cup (2 sticks) butter or margarine
2 cups sugar
5 egg yolks
2 cups sifted flour
1 teaspoon soda
1 cup buttermilk
1 teaspoon vanilla
1 small can coconut
1 cup chopped pecans
5 egg whites, beaten

Cream butter and sugar well. Add egg yolks, one at a time. Sift flour and soda together; add alternately with buttermilk. Add vanilla, coconut, and pecans. Fold in beaten egg whites. Pour into three greased 9-inch cake pans. Bake 40 minutes at 350°.

Frosting for Italian Cream Cake

1 8-ounce package cream cheese
½ cup margarine (1 stick)
1 pound confectioner's sugar
1 teaspoon vanilla
½ cup chopped nuts

Cream together cheese and margarine. Add sugar and vanilla, beating until smooth. Spread between layers and on top of cake. If stiff, add a little milk. Sprinkle nuts on top of cake.

Winter

Christmas Eve Fish Fest

Squid in Lemon Juice

Anchovy Dip and Celery

Tossed Green Salad

Della Robbia Gelatin Mold

Spinach in Tomato

Fettuccine with Basil

Stuffed Baked Squid

Shrimp with Sherry

Baked Trout

Salmon in Holiday Sauce

Baccala in White Wine

Assortment of Christmas Pastries

(Pita Piata, Pizzelles, Christmas Balls, Torrone Candy)

Christmas Dinner

Marinated Artichokes

Chicken Soup with Veal Meatballs

Green Salad

Turkey with Parmesan Dressing

Homemade Noodles

Green Beans Italiano

Christmas Pastries

Lemon Fruitcake

Fresh Fruit

Spring

A Calabrian Easter

Melon and Prosciutto

Tossed Salad

Ravioli

Baked Ham

Capon

Asparagus Parmesan

Easter Bread

Cassata

Lamb Cake

A Sicilian Easter

Steamed Artichokes

Chicken Soup with Saffron

Tiano (Traditional Egg and Noodle Dish)

Marinated Lamb

Green Salad

Cauliflower

Italian Cream Cake

Fruit

Summer

Fourth of July

Mushrooms Parmesan

Simple Shrimp Dip

Avocado Salad

Shiskabobs

Corn on the Cob, Roasted over Coals

Homemade Ice Cream

Watermelon

Family Reunion

Antipasto

Chicken Oregano

Melt-in-your-mouth Meatballs

Zucchini Tiella

Green Beans Italiano

Lasagna

Vienna Bread

Strawberry Ice

Pizzelles

Autumn

Homecoming Party

Sizzling Mushrooms in Olive Oil
Shrimp Dip
Tossed Salad
Mediterranean Paella
Fiesta Flank Steak
Crusty Bread
Cheesecake
Date Nut Ice Cream Cake

Fall Buffet

Spinach Balls
Tomatoes Stuffed with Herring
Stuffed Veal Breast
Turkey
Eggplant Parmesan
Broccoli
Fritta Rolls
Applesauce Cake
Instant Spumoni
Amaretto Chestnuts

Index

Appetizers

Beverages

Breads

Desserts and Party Foods

Egg and Cheese Dishes

Fishes

Fowl

Hot Sandwiches

Meat and Meat dishes

Pasta

Sauces

Salads

Soups

Vegetables